SERIES 3
FUTURES LICENSING EXAM REVIEW 2021
+ TEST BANK

SECURITIES INSTITUTE
SECURITIES LICENSING SERIES

The Securities Institute of America proudly publishes world class textbooks, test banks and video training classes for the following Financial Services exams:

Securities Industry Essentials exam / SIE exam
Series 3 exam
Series 4 exam
Series 6 exam
Series 7 exam
Series 9 exam
Series 10 exam
Series 22 exam
Series 24 exam
Series 26 exam
Series 39 exam
Series 57 exam
Series 63 exam
Series 65 exam
Series 66 exam
Series 99 exam

SERIES 3
FUTURES LICENSING EXAM REVIEW 2021 + TEST BANK

The National Commodities
Futures Examination

The Securities Institute of America, Inc.

ISBN: 978-1-937841-04-1

Printed in the United States of America.

10 9 8 7 6 5 4 3 2 1

Contents

CHAPTER 3
FUTURES PRICING   31

CHAPTER 4
PRICE FORECASTING   45

CHAPTER 7
CFTC & NFA AND REGULATIONS   143

About the Series 3 Exam

Congratulations! You are on your way to becoming licensed to transact business in commodity futures and options on futures. The Series 3 exam is a 120-question exam presented in both multiple-choice and true/false format. Each candidate will have 2 hours and 30 minutes to complete the exam. A score of 70% or higher is required on each of the two sections to pass. The Series 3 is as much a knowledge test as it is a reading test. The writers and instructors at The Securities Institute have developed the Series 3 textbook and exam prep software to ensure that you have the knowledge required to pass the test and that you are confident in your ability to apply that knowledge during the exam.

 IMPORTANT **EXAM NOTE!**

The Series 3 exam is one of the only exams that contains both multiple choice style questions and true / false style questions. The Series 3 also requires a passing score of 70% in each of the two sections of the test to pass the exam.

   To contact The Securities Institute of America, visit us on the Web at www.SecuritiesCE.com or call 877-218-1776.

TAKING THE SERIES 3 EXAM

The Series 3 exam is presented in multiple-choice format on a touch-screen computer known as the PROCTOR system. No computer skills are required, and candidates will find that the test screen works in the same way as an ordinary ATM machine. Each test is made up of 120 questions that are randomly chosen from a test bank of several thousand questions. The test has a time limit of 2 hours and 30 minutes, which is enough time for all candidates to complete the exam. Each Series 3 exam includes questions that focus on the following areas:

Part 1

- Futures Trading Theory and Futures Terminology—16 questions
- Futures Margins, Options Premiums, Price Limits, Settlements, Delivery, Exercise and Assignment—15 questions
- Types of Orders, Customer Accounts, Price Analysis—11 questions
- Basic Hedging and Hedging calculations—9 questions
- Financial Hedging—10 questions
- Spreading—3 questions
- Speculation in Commodity Futures, Financial Futures—16 questions
- Option Speculation, Hedging, and Spreading—5 questions

Part 2

- CFTC/NFA Rules and Regulations—35 Questions

HOW TO PREPARE FOR THE SERIES 3 EXAM

For most candidates, the combination of reading the textbook, watching the video class and taking as many practice questions as they can proves to be enough to successfully complete the exam. It is recommended that you spend at least 60 to 70 hours preparing for the exam by reading the textbook, underlining key points, and completing as many practice questions as possible. We recommend that students schedule the exam no more than 1 week after completing their Series 3 exam prep.

Test-Taking Tips

- Read the full question before answering.
- Identify what the question is asking.
- Identify key words and phrases.

- Watch out for hedge clauses, such as *except* and *not*.
- Eliminate wrong answers.
- Identify synonymous terms.
- Be wary of changing answers.

WHAT TYPE OF POSITIONS MAY A SERIES 3 REGISTERED PRINCIPAL HOLD?

Individuals who have passed the Series 3 exam may register as an associated person with an NFA member and may transact business in futures contracts. Individuals who have passed the Series 3 exam may apply for NFA membership as associated persons of any of the following:

- Sole proprietor
- Futures commission merchant (FCM)
- Retail foreign exchange dealer (RFED)
- Introducing broker (IB)
- Commodity pool operator (CPO)
- Commodity trading advisor (CTA)

WHAT SCORE IS REQUIRED TO PASS THE EXAM?

A score of 70% or higher is needed in each of the two sections to pass the Series 3 exam.

ARE THERE ANY PREREQUISITES FOR THE SERIES 3?

There are no prerequisites for the Series 3 exam.

HOW DO I SCHEDULE AN EXAM?

Ask your firm's compliance department to schedule the exam for you or to provide a list of test centers in your area. You are NOT required to be sponsored by a Financial Industry Regulatory Authority (FINRA) member firm prior to making an appointment. The Series 3 exam may be taken any day that the exam center is open.

WHAT MUST I TAKE TO THE EXAM CENTER?

A picture ID is required. All other materials will be provided, including a calculator and scratch paper.

HOW SOON WILL I RECEIVE THE RESULTS OF THE EXAM?

The exam will be graded as soon as you answer your final question and hit the "Submit for Grading" button. It will take only a few minutes to get your results. Your grade will appear on the computer screen, and you will be given a paper copy by the exam center.

About This Book

The writers and instructors at The Securities Institute have developed the Series 3 textbook, video classes and exam prep software to ensure that you have the knowledge required to pass the test, and to make sure that you are confident in the application of the knowledge during the exam. The writers and instructors at The Securities Institute are subject matter experts as well as Series 3 test experts. We understand how the test is written and our proven test-taking techniques can dramatically improve your results.

Each chapter includes notes, tips, examples, and case studies with key information; hints for taking the exam; and additional insight into the topics. Each chapter ends with a practice test to ensure you have mastered the concepts before moving onto the next topic.

About the Test Bank

This book is accompanied by a test bank of hundreds of questions to further reinforce the concepts and information presented here. The test bank is provided to help students who have purchased our book from a traditional bookstore or from an online retailer such as Amazon. If you have purchased this textbook as part of a package from our website containing the full version of the software, you are all set and simply need to use the login instructions that were emailed to you at the time of purchase. Otherwise to access the test bank please email your purchase receipt to sales@securitiesce.com and we will activate your account. This test bank provides a small sample of the questions and features that are contained in the full version of the exam prep software.

If you have not purchased the full version of the exam prep software with this book, we highly recommend it to ensure that you have mastered the knowledge required for your exam. To purchase the exam prep software for this exam, visit The Securities Institute of America online at www.securitiesce.com or call 877-218-1776.

About The Greenlight Guarantee

Quite simply, the Greenlight guarantee is as follows:
Pass our Greenlight exam within 5 days of your actual exam, and if you do not pass we will refund the money you paid to The Securities Institute. If you only have access to the Limited Test Bank through the purchase of this textbook, you may upgrade your online account for a small fee to include the Greenlight exam and receive the full benefits of our greenlight money back pass guarantee.

About The Securities Institute of America

The Securities Institute of America, Inc. Helps thousands of securities and insurance professionals build successful careers in the financial services industry every year. In more than 25 years we have helped students pass more than 250,000 exams.

Our securities training options include:

- Classroom training
- Private tutoring
- Interactive online video training classes
- State-of-the-art exam prep test banks
- Printed textbooks
- ebooks
- Real-time tracking and reporting for managers and training directors

As a result, you can choose a securities training solution that matches your skill level, learning style, and schedule. Regardless of the format you choose, you can be sure that our securities training courses are relevant, tested, and designed to help you succeed. It is the experience of our instructors and the quality of our materials that make our courses requested by name at some of the largest financial services firms in the world.

To contact The Securities Institute of America, visit us on the Web at www.securitiesce.com or call 877-218-1776.

Futures and Forwards

INTRODUCTION

While commodity futures contracts are seen by many market participants as strictly financial instruments, commodity futures contracts are truly an evolution of market efficiency. Commodity futures contracts have allowed the producer and user of commodities to operate their business more efficiently and to manage risk associated with changing prices.

THE SPOT MARKET

Before the development of financial instruments and contracts, commodities were bought and sold in cash transactions. The transactions between the producer or seller of the commodity and the user or buyer of the commodity took place in the cash or spot market. In the spot market the producer of the commodity would bring his crop to the marketplace and sell the wheat or corn to any buyer with cash in hand. The spot market gets its name from the fact that the commodity is delivered and paid for "on the spot." The producer of the commodity who has the commodity on hand is said to be long the cash commodity. If the grower of corn has 100,000 bushels of corn stored in their silo, the farmer (producer) is said to be long 100,000 bushels of cash corn. The user of the commodity who does not have the commodity on hand but who needs to acquire the cash commodity in order to produce their product or to conduct their business is said to be short the cash commodity. A grower of cattle who needs the corn to feed his cattle would be considered to be short cash corn because the grower does not have the corn on hand and needs the corn to conduct his business and to feed his cattle. Alternatively, someone who has a contractual obligation to deliver the underlying cash commodity but who does not own the cash commodity would also be considered to be short the cash commodity. If a U.S. exporter has contracted to deliver 50,000 bushels of corn to a cattle grower in Mexico in 120 days but has not acquired the 50,000 bushels of corn, the exporter would be considered to be short cash.

FORWARD CONTRACTS

The first advancement in commodity trading was the development of cash forward contracts or forwards. Forward contracts are privately negotiated contracts for the purchase and sale of a commodity or financial instrument. The first forward contracts were developed for agricultural commodities like wheat and corn. The establishment of forward contracts allowed the buyer and seller of commodities to lock in prices for a delivery date in the future. The forward contract gave both parties the ability to manage their businesses more efficiently. Farmers could now grow crops knowing that they had locked in a sale price for the crop. The forward contract also allowed the farmer to sell their crop without having to haul it to market, hoping there were buyers waiting with cash in hand. The buyer or users of the commodities through the use of a forward contract now knew that they had locked in the supply of the commodity to meet their demand at a set price. Both parties to the forward contract have an obligation to perform under the contract. The buyer is obligated to accept delivery of and pay for the commodity at the agreed-upon time and location. The seller is obligated to deliver the stated amount and quality of the commodity at the agreed-upon time and location. Because the terms and conditions for each forward contract are negotiated on an individual basis, it is extremely difficult to find another party to take over the obligation under the contract should circumstances change between the contract date and the delivery date. There is no secondary market for forward contracts. Another drawback to the forward contract is counterparty or performance risk. The individual counterparty risk is borne by both parties to the forward contract. For the seller or producer of the commodity it is the risk that the buyer will not be able to make payment or take delivery. For the buyer of the commodity the counterparty risk is that the farmer may not be able to produce or deliver the commodity. If one party defaults on their obligation to perform under a forward contract there is no entity to step in to ensure that the other party is made whole. In modern financial markets, forwards are often used in the currency markets by corporations and banks doing business internationally. If a corporation knows that it needs to make a payment for a purchase in foreign currency 3 months from now, the corporation can arrange to purchase the currency from a bank the day before the payment is due.

FUTURES

As the use of forward contracts evolved, the need to offset obligations through a secondary market and to eliminate counterparty risk led to the development of commodity futures contracts. Futures, like forwards, are a two-party contract. The specific terms and conditions of the contracts are standardized and set by the exchanges on which the futures contracts trade. The contract amount, delivery date, and type of settlement vary between the different types of futures contracts. Many futures contracts are an agreement for the delivery of a specific amount of a commodity at a specific place and time such as 5,000 bushels of wheat during the delivery period of the contract month. Futures began to trade for commodities such as wheat and gold and over the years have expanded to include financial futures such as futures on Treasury securities and most recently single stock futures. The standardized contract terms allows for a very liquid secondary market. The counterparty risk has been eliminated through performance guarantees. So even if one party to a contract defaults and does not meet their obligation, the other party will be made whole. Investors and hedgers can establish both long and short positions in commodity futures contracts. A person who has purchased the futures contract is long the contract, and until the buyer executes an offsetting sale the contract remains open. Alternatively a person who has sold the futures contract to open the position is considered to be short the futures contract, and until the seller closes out the contract with an offsetting purchase the contract remains open.

THE ROLE OF THE FUTURES EXCHANGE

The futures exchange at the most basic level provides a centralized location where buyers and sellers come together to transact business in futures. The exchange provides a centralized location where producers and users of commodities can lock in prices, manage their business, and hedge their risks. A farmer can lock in a sales price for his corn production by selling corn futures. A baking company may lock in a price for wheat by purchasing wheat futures. By engaging in futures transactions, the producer of corn and the buyer of wheat have both hedged their risk and can now operate their businesses more efficiently and without immediate concern over large price swings. The use of futures contracts has resulted in a reduction in business risk and commodity costs. These cost savings are passed along to the economy as buyers of the finished product enjoy the lower prices for finished goods like a loaf of bread. Additionally, because futures reduce the business risk to the producers and users of commodities, these companies are now able to obtain credit at lower rates. A lender reviewing the loan application of a farmer who grows corn will be more confident in making the loan if the lender knows that the farmer has locked in a sale price for his product. Finally, the exchange provides a place for risk capital to speculate on the direction of various commodities. These speculators provide a significant level of liquidity to the marketplace and make it easier for producers and users to hedge their business risk in the underlying cash commodity. These speculators are willing to assume the risk that producers and users want to eliminate.

TRADING FUTURES ON THE FLOOR OF THE EXCHANGE

Only individuals who own a membership on the exchange may conduct business on the floor of the exchange. A firm must be associated with an individual who owns a membership to qualify as a member firm. Futures exchanges, like other exchanges, are self-regulatory organizations and are responsible for establishing rules for their members and ensuring members adhere to just and equitable trade practices. The futures exchanges have the authority to investigate members and assess fines and penalties if the exchange finds that a member has violated its rules. The exchange establishes the margin requirements that must be deposited to establish a position for each futures contract. This is known as *original margin*. The exchange also establishes the minimum amount of equity or margin that must be maintained to continue to hold the position. This is known as *minimum maintenance margin*. Futures trading on the floor of the exchange takes place in the futures *pit* for the specific contract. For a long time trades for futures contracts were not allowed to take place away from the pit or outside the ring. While many securities listed on a stock exchange also trade in the over-the–counter (OTC) market, futures contracts were not traded OTC or off the floor. All trades were executed on the floor of the exchange in the pits. As the trades occur, the floor reporter would report the trades to the tape for dissemination to the marketplace. The report to the tape would be sent throughout the world to interested parties who transact business in futures contracts, much the same as a trade in the stock of an NYSE-listed company is disseminated. Orders for each type of futures contract would be directed to the pit for execution. Floor brokers and floor traders would come together in an open outcry market to announce their respective bids and offers for the contracts. A floor broker is an employee of a member organization and will execute orders for the member's customers and for the member's own account. A floor trader is a member of the exchange who trades for his or her own account. Floor traders are also known as locals or scalpers. These members stand in the pit to trade futures contracts for their own profit and loss. Some locals will simply day trade to make the spread on the contract or try to earn a quick profit on a small move in the price of the contract. The practice of day trading on small moves is the origin of the term *scalper*. Other floor traders will take positions overnight or for longer periods of time. These floor traders are known as position traders. Floor traders are not obligated to take on positions nor are they required to buy or sell in the absence of orders or if the spread in the contract price becomes excessive. The exchange's floor committee sets the rules for trading futures on the floor of the exchange and will resolve trading disputes between members. The CME Group which owns the Chicago Mercantile Exchange, the NYMEX, CBOT, and the KCBOT now allows approved firms to display bids and offers for contracts "on the screen" through CME globex electronic trading platform. Orders executed by firms with technology trading privileges will clear through the exchange as a futures contract.

The Globex platform provides electronic trading for futures and options in all asset classes. The CME Group through its Globex platform provides 24-hour trading. Firms may enter trades directly in the Globex platform and trade futures on a continuous basis. Firms with access to Globex are provided with real-time price data, risk management tools, and price discovery that allows for the viewing of open orders on the book.

CLEARINGHOUSE

All commodity exchanges must have a clearinghouse to clear all commodities futures transactions executed on the floor or clear through the exchange. The clearinghouse guarantees contract performance and eliminates all counterparty risk. If one party to a contract defaults the clearinghouse will ensure the financial performance of the contract, but not the actual delivery of the underlying commodity. All transactions in futures contracts are two-party contracts and each party accepts an obligation at the time the trade is executed. Neither the buyer nor seller of the contract knows the identity of the other party to whom they are now obligated. The clearinghouse is the ultimate counterparty for each buyer and each seller of futures contracts. If the buyer of a futures contract did not wish to take delivery of the underlying commodity, the buyer could simply offset his futures position with an offsetting sale of the contract. All offsetting transactions must be executed on the floor or clear through the same exchange and in the same futures contract month to close out the position.

EXAMPLE   A gold miner in Colorado who is concerned about the value of gold falling before the gold can be extracted sells a gold futures contract to a speculator in New York who believes that the price of gold is likely to increase in the next few weeks. Both the miner and speculator have now taken on an obligation to each other. The miner is obligated to deliver the gold and the speculator is obligated to purchase the gold. If the speculator determines that the price of gold is not likely to increase any further and does not want to accept delivery of the gold, the speculator would simply sell the gold contract. This offsetting transaction in no way affects the miner in Colorado who is still obligated to deliver the gold. The clearinghouse will assign the delivery to another market participant who is long the gold futures contract at the time the miner sends notice of intent to deliver the gold.

When a buyer or seller of a futures contract offsets his or her position they have effectively exited the market and are no longer obligated to any party.

Firms that transact business in commodity futures who are members of the clearinghouse will report all of their transactions to the clearinghouse. The clearinghouse will net the purchases and sales for all transactions executed during the trading session. Based on the trades that are reported to the clearinghouse by clearing member firms, the clearinghouse will calculate the original margin requirement that must be deposited by each member firm. Trades in futures contracts settle the next business day and the member firm must deposit the required margin by the open of the next trading day.

EXAMPLE   ABC commodities is a clearing firm member. During the course of the trading day ABC had customers establish new long positions in gold futures of 100 contracts. During the same trading day ABC also had customers who established new short positions in gold futures of 60 contracts. ABC would report to the clearinghouse that it had established 100 long contracts in gold futures and had established 60 short contracts in gold futures. The clearinghouse would then calculate the original margin that must be deposited by ABC commodities for these positions. Most clearinghouses will net the positions to determine the amount of original margin that must be deposited. In this case ABC customers went long 100 contracts while other ABC customers when short 60 contracts. If the clearinghouse nets the positions, ABC will only be required to deposit the original margin for 40 long gold contracts.

 TAKENOTE!

ABC would still be required to collect the original margin from its customers in the above example for all 100 long contracts and all 60 short contracts.

All commodities futures merchants must clear all transactions through the clearinghouse. The merchant may do this by becoming a member of a clearinghouse or the merchant may find it easier to have another clearinghouse member provide the clearing functions for its transactions and will pay the clearinghouse member a fee for this service.

CLEARING MEMBER MARGIN CALCULATIONS

Original margin refers to the amount that a member firm must deposit to establish a position in a futures contract. The amount of the original margin requirement is set by the exchange. Once the position has been established the clearinghouse will measure the amount of margin (equity) on deposit in relationship to the market price of the futures contract to determine if the position remains above the minimum maintenance for the contract. This process is known as *marking to the market*. As the price of the futures contract changes, the amount of margin on deposit will change in relation to the change in price of the futures contract. If the price of the futures contract moves against the member firm the amount of their margin deposit will be reduced. Should the contract move sufficiently against the firm, causing the deposit to fall below the minimum maintenance level, the clearinghouse will issue a call for additional or variation margin. A call for additional margin must be met by the next business day. When the clearinghouse marks to the market, the price for the contract is based on the official settlement price established and published by the exchange at the close of each trading day. In the rare event that no trades have taken place in a particular contract, the exchange will select the midpoint of the spread between the bid and the ask to determine a settlement price. During times of extreme volatility a clearinghouse could issue a call during the trading day for additional margin. In these extreme events a margin call issued during the trading day must be met within 1 hour.

Alternatively if a futures position moves in favor of the clearinghouse member, causing an increase in the margin (equity) on deposit for the contract to be in excess of the original margin requirement, the clearinghouse will send the excess back to the clearinghouse member.

Unlike a margin account for equities there is no loan being made to the customer and there is no debit balance or interest charged.

BASIS GRADE

The exchange sets a minimum standard for the quality of a commodity that may be delivered under the settlement of a futures contract. This standard is known as the basis grade for the commodity. Having a minimum quality standard ensures a buyer that he or she will receive a grade of commodity suitable for their needs. The basis grade also informs the seller or delivering party of the minimum quality that may be accepted for delivery under the contract. If a seller delivers a commodity in an inferior grade, the exchange may allow the seller to deliver the inferior or substitute grade at a discounted price to the buyer. Alternatively, if the seller delivers a substitute grade of the commodity that is superior to the basis grade, the seller may demand a premium upon delivery. The exchange will set limits as to what substitute grades (inferior and superior) may be delivered to settle futures contracts.

CORNERING THE MARKET

Futures exchanges will allow for the delivery of a substitute grade to settle a contract to help ensure that no one corners the market in any given commodity. If a person or group controls all or substantially all of a commodity, they are said to have cornered the market. While this is extremely hard to do, if accomplished, it could have significant consequences for not only market participants but for the economy as a whole. Should a group corner the cash market in a commodity, they would be able to demand almost any price for that commodity. Sellers of futures contracts would be forced to pay extraordinary prices for the underlying commodity to complete delivery, or they would be forced to offset or cover their short futures position at equally high prices

DELIVERY

The delivery process for each commodity is set by the exchange where the futures contract trades. The delivery of the underlying commodity is not delivered to the buyer but rather to a warehouse that has been approved by the exchange to accept delivery on behalf of all buyers. Once the seller deposits the commodity in the approved warehouse, that commodity will be inspected to make sure that it is in the proper grade and quantity. If the exchange has more than one approved delivery location the seller of the commodity will determine to which facility delivery will be made. The buyer of the commodity must accept delivery at whichever location the seller chooses. The buyer of the commodity has no authority to select the delivery location. Delivery may only take place during the contract month. For example, a seller who established a short position in June corn futures in April could not deliver the corn to settle the contract until the settlement period in June. The first day in a contract month when delivery may be made is known as the *first notice day*. A seller who wishes to deliver the commodity will notify his broker of the intention to deliver the commodity and the broker will in turn submit the notice of intention to deliver to the clearinghouse. The notice will contain specific details regarding the delivery including:

- The date when delivery will be made
- The location where delivery will be made
- The quantity or weight to be delivered
- The grade (basis, premium, or discount) to be delivered

Once the clearinghouse member receives the notice from the seller of the contract, the clearinghouse must determine which futures commission merchant with an established long position will be assigned the delivery notice to take delivery of the cash commodity. The method under which a notice is assigned to a buyer who is long futures varies from exchange to exchange. The notice may be assigned to the futures commission merchant with the oldest open long position or the largest net long position. The futures commission merchant will then assign the delivery notice to one of its customers with an open long position. The amount that the buyer will pay to the seller of the commodity is the settlement price on the day the seller filed the notice to deliver. Certain exchanges require that the buyer accept delivery of the commodity and do not allow the buyer to offset the delivery requirement by selling the same futures contract. This is known as a *stopped* delivery notice. Other exchanges will allow a person who is long the futures and who has been assigned a delivery notice to sell futures contracts in the same delivery month and pass or retender the delivery notice to the buyer. By selling the same futures in which the assigned party was long, the buyer has offset or eliminated the requirement to take delivery. The exchange will set a last trade day as the last day when a contract holder's obligations may be offset. Ultimately most contracts are offset and do not result in delivery.

SPECULATORS AND HEDGERS

The exchanges provide a liquid marketplace where both speculators and hedgers can readily transact futures trading. The role of the speculator is to take on the risk that the hedger is seeking to reduce or offset. The flow of risk capital to the futures markets allows the speculator to profit from a move in the futures market based on their belief about the price action in the commodity. A speculator who thinks that the price of the underlying commodity is likely to appreciate will purchase the futures contract to establish a long position. The long position will become profitable if the value of the futures contract appreciates. Alternatively, a speculator who feels that the price of the commodity is likely to fall will sell the futures contract to establish a short position. The short position will become profitable if the price of the commodity futures contract declines. A hedger who transacts business in futures contracts is seeking to manage or offset the price risk associated with either producing or using the commodity. A producer of the commodity who is long the cash commodity is seeking to protect the value or sales price of their inventory and is hedging against a price drop in the commodity. The producer would sell futures to hedge their long cash commodity position. Alternatively, a user or purchaser of the underlying commodity who is considered to be short the cash commodity is trying to protect their business from rising prices. In order to protect their business from a price increase in the underlying cash commodity, the user or purchaser of the commodity would buy futures. The hedger is not seeking to profit from trading futures, the hedger is simply looking to eliminate the risk of loss as the result of a move in the price of the underlying commodity.

Pretest

1. The minimum quality grade that may be delivered to fulfill the obligation of a futures contract is known as:

   a. Premium grade.

   b. Basis grade.

   c. Minimum grade.

   d. Standard grade.

2. Most exchange-traded futures contracts may be traded in the pit on the floor of the exchange or between dealers electronically.

   True
   False

3. Which of the following sets the rules for trading futures on the floor of the exchange and will resolve trading disputes between members?

   a. Floor committee

   b. NFA

   c. CFTC

   d. Floor official

4. Forward contracts are privately negotiated contracts for the purchase and sale of a commodity or financial instrument and offer a high degree of liquidity.

   True
   False

5. The transactions between the producer or seller of the commodity and the user or buyer of the commodity take place in the
   a. Forward market.
   b. Futures market.
   c. Exchange market.
   d. Spot market.

6. The counterparty risk in all futures contracts has been eliminated through performance guarantees.
   True
   False

7. The delivery process for each commodity is set by the exchange where the futures contract trades. The delivery of the underlying commodity is delivered to:
   a. The buyer.
   b. The exchange.
   c. An approved clearinghouse.
   d. An approved warehouse.

8. A seller who wishes to deliver the commodity will notify his broker of the intention to deliver the commodity and the broker will in turn submit the notice of intention to deliver to the clearinghouse. The notice will contain all of the following EXCEPT:
   a. The date when delivery will be made.
   b. A margin release form.
   c. The location where delivery will be made.
   d. The quantity or weight to be delivered.

9. All investors with open long positions who receive a delivery notice may offset the delivery by selling the futures contract and tendering the delivery notice to the new buyer.
   True
   False

10. A seller who wishes to deliver the commodity may notify his broker of the intention to deliver the commodity on:

    a. The first delivery day.

    b. The week prior to the delivery month.

    c. The last business day of the preceding month.

    d. The first notice day.

Trading Commodity Futures

INTRODUCTION

Investors who wish to trade futures contracts will have their orders routed to the specific exchange, to a specific pit, or displayed electronically to establish or to offset a position in any particular futures contract. The market participants all have very different reasons for trading commodity futures contracts and will each use a variety of trading strategies to meet their market objectives. Just as each market participant has different reasons for trading futures, there are a number of different types of orders that each may use to establish or to exit a futures position. We will begin by looking at the types of orders that an investor may enter and the reasons for entering the various types of orders. Series 3 candidates can expect to see a number of questions on trading futures contracts.

TYPES OF ORDERS

Orders entered to buy or sell commodity futures contracts are all entered to buy or sell a specific number of contracts in the stated contract month. Investors can enter various types of orders to buy or sell futures. Some orders guarantee that the investor's order will be executed immediately. Other types of orders may state a specific price or condition under which the investor wants their order to be executed. All orders are considered *day* orders unless otherwise specified. All day orders will be canceled at the end of the trading day if they are not executed. An investor may also specify that their order remain active until canceled. This type of order is known as *good 'til cancel* or *GTC*.

MARKET ORDERS

A market order will guarantee that the investor's order is executed as soon as the order is presented to the market. A market order to either buy or sell guarantees the execution, but not the price at which the order will be executed. When a market order is presented for execution, the market for the contract may be very different from the market that was displayed when the order was entered. As a result, the investor does not know the exact price at which their order will be executed. An investor may enter a market order to purchase crude oil such as:

Buy 3 June crude oil MKT

An investor who has entered the above order to purchase 3 June crude oil contracts at the market does not know what price he will pay for the contracts when the order reaches the market.

BUY LIMIT ORDERS

A buy limit order sets the maximum price that the investor will pay for the futures contract. The order may never be executed at a price higher than the investor's limit price. While a buy limit order guarantees that the investor will not pay over a certain price, it does not guarantee an execution. If the futures contract continues to trade higher away from the investor's limit price, the investor will not purchase the futures contract and may miss a chance to realize a profit from establishing a long position or may have to pay more for the contract when offsetting a short position. An investor who wants to purchase corn may enter a limit order to purchase corn as follows:

Buy 2 December corn @1.40

The investor wants to purchase 2 December corn contracts at a maximum price of 1.40. If the market for December corn is above 1.40 when the order reaches the market, the order will only be executed if the futures contract trades down to the investor's limit price of 1.40, otherwise the order will not be executed.

SELL LIMIT ORDERS

A sell limit order sets the minimum price that the investor will accept for the futures contract. The order may never be executed at a price lower than the investor's limit price. While a sell limit order guarantees that the investor will not receive less than a certain price, it does not guarantee an execution. If the futures contract continues to trade lower away from the investor's limit price, the investor will not sell the futures contract and may miss a chance to realize a profit from establishing a short position or may receive less for the contract when offsetting a long position. An investor who wants to sell wheat may enter a limit order as follows:

Sell 5 September wheat 1.52

The investor wants to sell 5 September wheat contracts at a minimum price of 1.52. If the market for September wheat is below 1.52 when the order reaches the market, the order will only be executed if the futures contract trades up to the investor's limit price of 1.52, otherwise the order will not be executed.

 FOCUS**POINT!**

It's important to remember that even if an investor sees futures contracts trading at their limit price, it does not mean that their order was executed, because there could have been other orders for futures contracts ahead of them at that limit price.

 TAKE**NOTE!**

Limit orders are sometimes referred to as resting orders due to the fact that the limit price of the orders are often away from the market.

STOP ORDERS/STOP LOSS ORDERS

A stop order or stop loss order can be used by investors to limit or guard against a loss, or to protect a profit. A stop order will be placed away from the market in case the futures contract starts to move against the investor. A stop order is not a *live* order; it has to be elected. A stop order is elected and becomes a live order when the futures contract trades at or through the stop price. The stop price is also known as the trigger price. Once the futures contract has traded at or through the stop price, the order becomes a market order to either buy or sell the futures contract depending on the type of order that was placed.

TAKE**NOTE**

Stop orders for futures contracts may be elected without a trade taking place. A sell stop order may also be elected if the futures contract is offered at or through the stop price. A buy stop order may also be elected if the futures contract is bid at or through the stop price.

BUY STOP ORDERS

A buy stop order is placed above the market and is used to protect against a loss or to protect a profit on a short sale of futures contracts. A buy stop order could also be used by a technical analyst to get long the futures contract after the futures contract breaks through resistance.

EXAMPLE   An investor has sold 10 June crude oil futures contracts at 81.25 to establish a short position. The June contract for crude oil has declined to 80.05. The investor is concerned that if the contract goes higher than 80.15 it may return to 81 very quickly. To protect their profit they enter an order to buy 10 June crude oil contracts at 80.20 stop. If crude trades at or through 80.20 the order will become a market order to buy 10 contracts and the investor will cover their short and by offsetting their short position at the next available price. The order in this case would be entered as follows:

Buy 10 June crude oil @ 80.20 stop

SELL STOP ORDERS

A sell stop order is placed below the market and is used to protect against a loss or to protect a profit on the purchase of a futures contract. A sell stop order could also be used by a technical analyst to get short the futures contract after the futures contract breaks through support.

EXAMPLE   An investor has purchased 10 May silver futures contracts at 15.50. The contract has risen to 17.10. The investor is concerned that if May silver falls below 17 it may return to 16 very quickly. To protect their profit they enter an order to sell 10 May silver at 16.90 stop. If May silver trades at or through 16.90, the order will become a market order to sell 10 May futures contracts and the investor will sell the futures contracts and offset their long position at the next available price. The order in this case would be entered as follows:

Sell 10 May silver at 16.90 stop

If in the same example the order to sell 10 May silver contracts at 16.90 stop was entered GTC, we could have a situation such as the following.

May silver closes at 17.40. The following morning the Federal Reserve Board announces that it plans to increase interest rates and to tighten the money supply, causing the U.S. dollar to rally sharply. As result, all the metals are indicated to open sharply lower. May silver opens at 16.45. The opening print of 16.45 elected the order and the futures contract would be sold on the opening or as close to the opening as practical.

STOP LIMIT ORDERS

An investor would enter a stop limit order for the same reasons they would enter a stop order. The only difference is that once the order has been elected the order becomes a limit order instead of a market order. The same risks that apply to traditional limit orders apply to stop limit orders. If the futures contract continues to trade away from the investor's limit, they could give back all of their profits or suffer large losses. The investor in the above silver contracts could have entered the stop order as a stop limit order as follows

Sell 10 May silver at 16.90 stop 16.85 limit. GTC

In this case, the investor is saying that they want to sell the contracts if May silver trades down to 16.90, but in no case will they accept less than 16.85. In the situation where silver gapped down in price on the open after the Federal Reserve's announcement, the investor would have had their stop order elected on the opening print of 16.45. However, their order would not be executed and it would be a limit order to sell May silver at 16.85. If silver continues to trade lower, the market will be further away from the investor's limit order and the investor could suffer large losses as a result.

OTHER TYPES OF ORDERS

There are several other types of orders that an investor may enter. They are:

- All or none (AON)
- Immediate or cancel (IOC)

- Fill or kill (FOK)
- Not held (NH)
- Disregard the tape (DRT)
- Market on open/market on close (MOO/MOC)
- Limit or market on close
- Market if touched
- One order cancels the other
- Cancels former order
- Switch order
- Scale order
- Basis order
- Exchange-for-physical order
- Bunched order
- Give-up order

All-or-none orders: May be entered as day orders or GTC. All-or-none orders, as the name implies, indicate that the investor wants to buy or sell all of the futures or none of them. AON orders are not displayed in the market because of the required special handling, and the investor will not accept a partial execution.

Immediate-or-cancel orders: The investor wants to buy or sell as many futures contracts as they can immediately, and whatever contracts cannot be cannot be filled are canceled.

Fill-or-kill orders: The investor wants the entire order executed immediately and all contracts covered in the order must be bought or sold. If all contracts in the order cannot be executed, the entire order is canceled.

Not-held orders or disregard tape (NH/DRT): The investor gives discretion to the floor broker as to the time and price of execution. All retail not-held orders given to a representative are considered day orders unless the order is received in writing from the customer and entered GTC.

Market on open: The investor wants their order executed on the opening of the market or as reasonably close to the opening as practical. The exchange sets an opening time range that is considered to be the open of the trading day. All orders executed during this time will be considered to have been executed on the open. If the order is not executed during this time, it is canceled. Limit orders and partial executions are allowed for these orders. A market on open would be noted as follows:

Buy 2 June crude market opening only

In this case the broker will buy 2 June crude contracts at whatever price is available during the opening range of the market.

A limit on open would be noted as follows:

Buy 2 June crude at 81.20 opening only

In this case the broker will buy 2 June crude contracts only if a price of 81.20 or better is available during the opening range of the market. If the order cannot be executed it will be canceled at the expiration of the market-on-open period.

Market on close: The investor wants their order executed on the closing of the market or as reasonably close to the close as practical. The exchange sets a closing time range that is considered to be the close of the trading day. All orders executed during this time will be considered to have been executed on the close. If the order is not executed during this time, it is canceled. Limit orders and partial executions are allowed for these orders. A market on close would be noted as follows:

Sell 2 June crude market closing only

In this case the broker will sell 2 June crude contracts at whatever price is available during the closing range of the market.

A limit on close would be noted as follows:

Sell 2 June crude at 81.50 closing only

In this case the broker will sell 2 June crude contracts only if a price of 81.50 or better is available during the closing range of the market. If the order cannot be executed it will be canceled at the expiration of the market on closing period.

Limit or market on close: With this type of order the investor wants their order executed during the trading session at their limit price or better. However, if the order has not been executed during the trading session the investor wants the order to turn into a market order to purchase or sell the contracts on the closing of the market or as reasonably close to the close as practical during the closing time range set by the exchange. A limit or market on close order would be entered as follows:

Sell 10 May silver at 17.10 or market on close

In the above order the investor wants to sell the 10 May silver contracts at a price of 17.10 or better, but if they have not been sold at that price during the trading day the investor wants the 10 contracts sold at the market on the close of trading.

Market if touched (MIT): With this type of order the investor wants the order to be executed if the market trades at or through a set price. Unlike a limit order, the MIT order becomes a market order to purchase or sell the contracts at the next available price. An MIT order to buy futures contracts would be entered below the market and would be elected if the futures contract trades at or through or is offered at the trigger price. An MIT order to buy futures may be entered as follows:

Buy 5 September wheat at 1.50 MIT

The above order will be executed at the market if September wheat trades at 1.50 or lower or if September wheat is offered at 1.50. A buy order entered as a market-if-touched order could be used by an investor who wishes to establish a long position or by an investor who is looking to offset a short position.

An MIT order to sell futures contracts would be entered above the market and would be elected if the futures contract trades at or through or is bid at the trigger price. An MIT order to sell futures may be entered as follows:

Sell 8 September corn at 1.75 MIT

The above order will be executed at the market if September corn trades at 1.75 or higher or if September corn is bid at 1.75. A sell order entered as a market-if-touched order could be used by an investor who wishes to establish a short position or by an investor who is looking to offset a long position. An order that is entered as a market-if-touched order is also known as a board order.

One order cancels the other (OCO): This order is entered as one order with two orders to trade a futures contract. If one order is executed, the other order is automatically canceled. For example an investor who is long 5 September wheat contracts at 1.50 when September wheat is trading at 1.55 may enter the following OCO order:

Sell 5 September wheat at 1.60 or sell 5 September wheat at 1.50 stop

In this case the investor is trying to sell the wheat at 1.60 and realize a profit. However, the investor does not want to suffer a loss on the position and has entered a sell stop as part of the order at 1.50. If wheat rallies from 1.55 to 1.60 the investor will sell 5 September wheat contracts at that price and the stop order to sell the 5 September wheat contracts at 1.50 will be canceled. Alternatively, if September wheat falls back to 1.50 the stop order will be elected and the investor will sell the wheat at or around 1.50. Once the stop order to sell the contracts at 1.50 is elected and filled, the limit order to sell the September wheat at 1.60 would be canceled.

Cancels former order (CFO): This order is entered when an investor wishes to change the terms of an existing order. An investor may be making a change to a limit price, the number of contracts, or may be changing the order from a day order to a GTC order. A CFO may be entered as follows:

Buy 4 September silver at 16.50
CFO Buy 4 September silver at 16.30

Switch order: This order is entered when an investor wishes to change or roll the delivery month of an existing position into a position in a different delivery month. For example, an investor who is long 1 June crude oil contract may not wish to accept delivery of 5,000 barrels of crude oil in June but believes that the price of crude will continue to appreciate, so may enter a switch order as follows:

Sell 1 June crude 81.60
Buy 1 December crude 82.30

The above order rolls the investor's obligation to accept delivery of the crude oil from June forward into December by offsetting the long June contract with the sale and by establishing a new long position in the December contract.

> ▶ TAKE**NOTE!**
>
> Because a switch order contains two contract months or legs and is the simultaneous execution of two futures contracts, the customer will be charged a full round-turn commission to execute a switch order.

Scale order: This order is entered when an investor wishes to establish or offset a position by purchasing or selling futures contracts at specified intervals. This will allow an investor to establish or liquidate a position at an average price instead of just executing the full order at a prevailing price in case the market moves against the investor. A scale order may be entered as follows:

Buy 1 December S&P 500 1652.00 and buy 19 additional contracts every 5 points lower

In the above scale order the investor is seeking to purchase a total of 20 S&P 500 contracts. Instead of purchasing the contracts all at the current price of 1652, the investor has purchased one contract at the current market price of 1652 and will buy one additional contract every 5 points until the total of 20 contracts has been purchased. In this case the investor will purchase an additional contract at 1647, 1642, and so on.

Basis order (contingent order): This order is entered when an investor wishes to establish or liquidate a position by purchasing or selling futures contracts based on or contingent upon certain market events. A basis order may be entered by an investor to execute the order if the spread between two contract months for the same commodity reaches a certain range. A basis order could be entered as follows:

If May corn trades at 1.60 buy 10 December corn at 1.68.

In this case the investor wants to pay 8 cents over the May corn contract price to purchase 10 December corn contracts if the May corn contract trades at 1.60 or higher. A basis order may also be entered to purchase or sell futures contracts based upon trading in other related commodities. An investor who trades silver may wish to buy or sell silver based on the price action of gold. An investor may enter a basis order of this type as follows:

If June gold trades at 1600 buy 10 June silver at 17.80.

Exchange-for-physical order (EFP): This is the only type of order that may take place off the screen and outside of the trading pit on the floor of the exchange. An EFP order consists of the exchange of the physical underlying cash commodity for a futures contract. This type of order could take place between a producer and user of the commodity. The producer who is long the commodity and short futures will agree to deliver the physical commodity to the user of the commodity who is long the futures contract in exchange for the user's long futures contract. This type of off-the-floor exchange is also known as an ex-pit transaction.

Bunched order: A bunched order is usually executed by an advisory firm or commodity pool operator for the accounts of a number of clients. The advisory firm will enter a single large order and will then allocate the contracts to client accounts.

EXAMPLE

An advisory firm who thinks that the stock market is likely to rise over the next few months wants to position a group of clients in S&P 500 futures. The firm may enter an order to purchase 200 December S&P 500 futures contracts for these clients and will allocate the contracts accordingly.

 TAKENOTE!

The allocation to clients does not have to be made prior to execution, but the allocation must be completed by the end of the trading day.

Give-up order: A client who wishes to remain anonymous may ask their futures commission merchant (FCM) to give the order out to another FCM for execution to protect their identity. This would usually only be done in cases where, if the name of the client or firm was known in the marketplace, it would adversely impact the ability to execute the order. For example, if the market knew that a very large and very well respected commodities firm was shorting gold futures, the market participants would likely try to sell gold futures down to get on the same side of the market as the well-regarded commodities firm. By executing the order under the name of another FCM, the client or firm has remained anonymous. The FCM that receives the order and the FCM who executes the order will split the commissions on the order.

COMMISSIONS

Traditionally commodity futures merchants charge customers a commission to execute orders based on a round turn rate. The round turn fee to be paid by the customer covers the opening of the position as well as the offset or closing transaction. Most round turn rates are charged based on the number of contracts included in the order.

EXAMPLE

A customer of XYZ, a futures commission merchant who charges a commission of $50 per round turn, executes the following order:

Buy 1 December S&P 500 @1745

The customer would be charged a total of $50 (or $25 per side) to purchase and sell the S&P 500 contract.

If the customer placed an order to purchase 10 contracts as follows:

Buy 10 December S&P 500 @1745

The customer would be charged a total of $500 (or $250 per side) to purchase and sell the 10 S&P 500 contracts.

Commission rates vary among commission merchants based on the level of services provided as well as by the type of orders entered. Orders that require the simultaneous execution of two futures contracts or sides may charge the customer a reduced round-trip rate for each side of the trade. This is often the case for spread transactions. Should the customer wish to roll out the delivery month to continue holding a position in the underlying commodity, the customer may enter a switch order. An example of a switch order for a customer long March corn would be as follows:

Buy 1 May corn
Sell 1 March corn

In the above trade the customer has purchased May corn and sold his long March corn contract to eliminate the requirement to take delivery of corn in March and to keep his long exposure to corn. The commission for the switch order would traditionally be the full round-turn rate as the customer has established a new position in a later month that will need to be offset at some point in the future.

DELIVERY MONTHS

The exchanges on which each futures contract trades set the available delivery months for the commodity futures contract. The exchange will establish delivery months for the commodities based upon the needs of the marketplace. In the case of agricultural commodities, the contract months will be based upon the needs of producers and users of the commodities. Many agricultural commodities contracts are based upon the crop year for the commodity. Futures contracts do not trade with delivery in all calendar months. If contracts traded for delivery in all months, the market for each contract would be too thin to offer proper pricing and liquidity. Most futures contracts trade with the distant month expirations between 12 and 18 months out. Futures contracts will be listed by the commodity and the delivery month, with the nearest-term delivery month quoted first and progressing to more distant delivery months.

The following table shows the quote for March and May corn futures.

Corn	Last	Change	Prior Settlement	High	Low	Volume	Hi/lo Limit
March	423'2	−2'0	425'4	426'4	420'4	95,100	465.4/385'4
May	431'4	−2'0	433'6	434'6	428'4	25,100	473'6/393'6

The following table shows the symbols for the contract months.

Month	Symbol	Month	Symbol
January	F	July	N
February	G	August	Q
March	H	September	U
April	J	October	V
May	K	November	X
June	M	December	Z

The following table shows the open outcry symbols for some of the more actively traded contracts.

Contract	Symbol	Contract	Symbol
Corn	C	RBOB Gasoline	RB
Soybean	S	Gold	GC
Wheat	W	Silver	SI
Sugar	SU	Copper	HG
Feeder Cattle	FC	S&P 500	SP
Live Cattle	LC	S&P Mini	ES
Lean Hogs	LH	U.S. Treasury Bond	US
Light Sweet Crude	CL	Eurodollar	ED
Natural Gas	NG	Japanese Yen	JY

Pretest

1. Which of the following is true as it relates to buy stop orders?

    a. A buy stop order is placed below the market.

    b. A buy stop order would be used to protect a profit on a long futures contract.

    c. A buy stop order is placed above the market.

    d. A buy stop order can be used to offset a long contract.

2. A market on open order will be executed:

    a. On the opening print only.

    b. Within the opening time range.

    c. Only during the first five trades.

    d. At a price equal to the opening price.

3. Which of the following orders will have a life expectancy greater than a few seconds after the order is presented to the market?

    a. All or none

    b. Market order

    c. Immediate or cancel

    d. Fill or kill

4. Unlike a limit order, the MIT order becomes a market order to purchase or sell the contracts at the next available price when the trigger price is reached.

    True
    False

5. An investor who has an open order to purchase a futures contract that is trading higher and away from their limit price wants to increase the price on his open order. What type of order would the investor enter?

   a. Switch order

   b. AON

   c. CFO

   d. IOC

6. A silver and gold trader enters the following order. If October gold trades at 1320 sell 10 October silver at 19.20. What type of order is this?

   a. FCO

   b. Switch order

   c. Basis order

   d. Scale order

7. Which of the following orders would be used by a large investor who wishes to keep their identity from being known?

   a. Sale order

   b. Switch order

   c. Give-up order

   d. Broker order

8. This order is entered when an investor wishes to establish or offset a position by purchasing or selling futures contracts at specified intervals.

   a. Bunched

   b. Scale

   c. FCO

   d. Switch

9. A DRT order gives discretion to the floor broker as to the time and price of execution.

   True
   False

Futures Pricing

INTRODUCTION

Each commodities futures contract has specific pricing characteristics that are set by the exchange and designed to reflect the needs of the market participants who use the commodity. The amount of the underlying commodity covered in a futures contract, the pricing increments, and the expiration months traded are all established with the production and use of the commodity in mind.

CONTRACT SIZES AND PRICING

Each commodities futures contract represents a stated amount of the underlying commodity and is priced in increments that reflect the price per unit of the underlying commodity. For example, a corn contract represents 5,000 bushels of corn and is priced in cents per bushel. Alternatively a gold futures contract that covers 100 troy ounces of gold is priced in dollars and cents per troy ounce. One troy ounce is equal to 1.09714 ounces. The exchange on which the futures contract trades also sets the minimum price variation for the contract, known as a tick. The value of each tick per contract is based upon the pricing of the contract and upon the number of units of the underlying commodity covered by the contract. For the corn and gold contracts above the pricing and value of the tick would be as follows:

Corn tick = ¼ of 1 cent per bushel = $0.0025 × 5,000 bushels = $12.50 per contract

Gold tick = 10 cents per troy ounce = $.10 × 100 troy ounces = $10 per contract

In addition to setting the minimum price variation per contract, the exchange also sets a maximum amount by which the value of the contract may change during a trading session. This is known as limit up—limit down or the daily price limit. Most contracts have a stated amount by which the contract can raise or fall from the previous day's settlement price. However, the current or spot month is usually not subject to a daily price limit. The limit up and limit down rule is designed to keep the market for the underlying commodity stable and to avoid panics. Most contracts have initial limits that can be expanded during times of heightened volatility at the discretion of the exchange. Should three or more contract delivery months close limit up or limit down for a given commodity, the Chicago Board of Trade (CBOT) may expand the daily price limit to 150% of the standard daily price limit. These expanded daily price limits will remain in effect for 3 consecutive trading days. If the daily price limit is increased for a given commodity due to extreme volatility in order to protect the clearinghouse, commodity merchants, and customers, the CBOT will automatically increase the minimum margin required to hold those contracts to 150% of the original minimum. The Chicago Mercantile Exchange (CME) does not automatically increase the margin requirement when the daily price limit expands. When a contract enters a state of limit up or limit down the contract will be said to be locked limit if no trades can take place within the limit price. At the point where the contract enters a lock limit state no trades will be executed.

EXAMPLE   The value of the corn contract has an initial daily price limit of 40 cents per bushel, which can be expanded to 60 cents per bushel when the market closed at limit bid or limit offer. On the other hand, the gold futures contract currently has no set daily price limit.

 TAKE**NOTE!**

The daily price limits for a given commodity contract are established by the board of directors at the exchange where the futures contract trades. All daily price limits set by the exchange are subject to review and approval of the Commodity Futures Trading Commission (CFTC).

The following table details the contract specifics for a number of actively traded commodity futures contracts.

Contract	Units	Pricing	Tick	Daily Price Limit	Delivery Months
Corn	5,000 Bushels	Cents per bushel	$.0025 per bushel $12.50 per contract	40 cents expandable to 60 cents	March, May, July, September, December
Soybean	5,000 Bushels	Cents per bushel	$.0025 per bushel $12.50 per contract	7% of the contract based on the 45-day average closing price reset every six months	January, March, May, July, August, September, November
Wheat	5,000 Bushels	Center per bushel	$.0025 per bushel 12.50 per contract	60 cents	March, May, July, September, December
Sugar	112,000 pounds	Dollars per pound	$.0001 per pound $11.20 per contract	No limit	March, May, July, and October
Feeder Cattle	50,000 pounds	Cents per pound	$.00025 per pound $12.50 per contract	.03 per pound	January, March, April, May, August, September, October, November
Live Cattle	40,000 pounds	Cents per pound	$.00025 per pound $10 per contract	.03 per pound	February, April, June, August, October, December
Lean Hogs	40,000 pounds	Cents per pound	$.00025 per pound $10 per contract	.03 per pound	February, April, May, June, July, August, October, December
Light Sweet Crude	1,000 barrels	Dollars and cents per barrel	$.01 per barrel $10 per contract	$10 per barrel	Consecutive months for the current year and next 5 years
Natural Gas	10,000 million BTUs	Dollars and cents per million BTUs	.001 per million BTUs $10 per contract	$1.50 per million BTUs	118 consecutive months
RBOB Gasoline	42,000 Gallons	Dollars and cents per gallon	$0.0001 per gallon $4.20 per contract	$.25 per gallon	36 consecutive months
Gold	100 troy ounces	Dollars and cents per troy ounce	$.10 per troy ounce $10 per contract	No limit	Current and next two months and February, April, August, and October

(Continued)

Contract	Units	Pricing	Tick	Daily Price Limit	Delivery Months
Silver	5,000 troy ounces	Cents per troy ounce	$0.005 per troy ounce $25 per contract	No limit	Current calendar month; the next 23 calendar months; and, March, May, July, September, December for 60 months
Copper	25,000 ponds	Cents per pound	$0.0005 per pound $12.50 per contract	No limit	24 consecutive calendar months
S&P 500	$250 × S&P 500 Index	U.S. dollar and cents	0.10 index points = $25 per contract	7%, 13% 20%	March, June, September, December
S&P Mini	$50 × S&P 500 Index	U.S. dollar and cents	0.10 index points = $25 per contract	7%, 13% 20%	March, June, September, December
U.S. Treasury bond	1 $100,000 par bond	Points ($1,000) and 1/32 of a point	One thirty-second (1/32) of one point ($31.25)	96/32 or $3,000 per contract. Expandable to 144/32 or $4,500 per contract	The first three consecutive contracts in the March, June, September, and December quarterly cycle.
Euro	125,000 Euros	Cents per Euro	$.0001 per euro increments ($12.50/ contract).	No limit	March, June, September, December
Japanese yen	12,500,000 Yen	Cents per Yen	$.000001 per Japanese yen increments ($12.50/ contract).	None l No limit	March, June, September, December

U.S. TREASURY FUTURES

Futures contracts covering a variety of U.S. Treasury obligations are traded on the CBOT. Although the futures contracts cover U.S. Treasury obligations, which are backed by the full faith and credit of the U.S. Government, the futures contracts are not backed by the U.S. Government. The futures contracts represent an obligation to the parties to the contract and are in no way obligations of the U.S. Government. The most widely traded contract is the U.S. T-bond contract. The futures contract covers $100,000 par value of U.S. Treasury bonds maturing at least 15 years from delivery date. In addition to a maturity date of at least 15 years, if the bonds have a call provision attached to them the bonds must not be callable within the first 15 years. U.S. Treasury futures contracts are quoted as a percentage of $100,000 par value in increments of 1/32 of 1%. 1/32 of 1% of $100,000 par value is equal to $31.25. A quote for the U.S. T-bond futures contract of 105.16 would translate in to a price as follows:

105.16 = 105 16/32% = 105.5% × $100,000 = $105,500

 TAKENOTE!

The price of U.S. Treasury futures moves inversely to the change in interest rates. Therefore an investor who felt interest rates were likely to rise would sell U.S. Treasury bond futures. Alternatively an investor who felt interest rates were likely to fall would purchase U.S. Treasury bond futures.

Futures contracts also trade on short-term U.S. Government obligations. The futures contract covering the 3-month T-bill is the most active contract. The U.S. T-bill contract covers $1,000,000 par value and is priced based upon an index as a discounted percentage from par. The price of the contract is determined by subtracting the interest rate from 100. If interest rates in the marketplace are currently at 3.25%, the price of the contract would be determined as follows:

100 − 3.25 = 96.75

If an investor felt interest rates were going to rise from 3.25% to 4%, the investor would sell the T-bill futures. If rates did indeed increase from 3.25% to 4%, the price of the T-bill contract would fall from 96.75 to 96.00.

The minimum increment change for a T-bill contract is 1 basis point or 0.01%. The basis point represents an annual interest rate. To determine the dollar value of 1 basis point for a T-bill futures contract, the value must be adjusted for the fact that the T-bill contract covers a three-month T-bill as follows:

.0001 × $1,000,000 = $100

$100 ÷ 4 = $25

In the above example, if rates rose from 3.25% to 4% and the contract price fell from 96.75 to 96 and the investor covered his short position at 96, the investor would have made $1,875 (75bps × $25).

 TAKENOTE!

Additional futures contracts trade on long-term instruments like Government National Mortgage Association (GNMAs) and Treasury notes. Additional short-term futures trade on Eurodollar deposits, domestic CDs, and Federal Funds.

STOCK INDEX FUTURES

The development of futures contracts for the major stock indexes has evolved into one of the most liquid futures markets. Futures contracts for the S&P 500 index, often referred to simply as S&Ps, are the premier contract. This highly liquid market allows investors to gain exposure to a broad basket of stocks representative of the overall market by simply placing an order to buy or sell S&P 500 futures contracts. The contract value of the S&P 500 is $250 times the contract price. If the S&P 500 contract is trading at 1625, the total contract value is $250 × 1625 = $406,250. One S&P point is worth $250. The contracts trade in minimum increments of $.10, with each tick worth $25. An investor who thinks that the overall market will advance may purchase S&P 500 contracts to gain exposure to the overall market in an attempt to profit from this belief. An investor who believes that the S&P 500 would advance from 1625 to 1700 enters the following order:

Buy 1 March S&P 500 at 1625

If the S&P does indeed increase from 1625 to 1700, the investor has made 75 points or $18,750 per contract. The profit per contract is found by multiplying the 75-point increase by the value of each point. Each S&P point is worth $250.

Alternatively an investor who felt the S&P 500 was likely to decline may enter an order to sell March S&P 500 contract at 1625:

Sell 1 March S&P 500 at 1625

If the S&P contract fell from 1625 to 1610.50, the investor would have made 14.50 points or $3,625 per contract. The profit per contract is found by multiplying the 14.50 point decrease by the value of each point. Each S&P point is worth $250.

INDEX FUTURE SETTLEMENT

The value of S&P futures contracts is based on an index value, which is calculated based on the price of the 500 stocks contained in the S&P 500 index. The S&P 500 contract settles in cash and not with the delivery of shares of the 500 companies. During the delivery month, a person who is long the S&P 500 futures contract will have their account credited, while a person who is short the S&P 500 contract will have their account debited. The difference between the price where the futures position was opened and where the contract expired will determine if the investor has made or lost money.

SINGLE STOCK FUTURES

Futures contracts on individual securities or single stock futures have been created for many of the most widely traded large cap stocks. Like other futures contracts single stock futures obligate both parties to either make or take delivery of the underlying instrument. The traditional contract size for single stock futures contracts is for 100 shares of the underlying security. Some single stock futures contracts may cover larger amounts for up to 1,000 shares of the underlying security. The CME Group and The Chicago Board Option Exchange (CBOE) created OneChicago to trade single stock futures contracts. The listing requirements for single stock futures contracts are regulated by both the Securities Exchange Commissions/SEC and The CFTC. The listing requirements require surveillance procedures to be in place to guard against insider trading in the underlying security. The trading volume in the underlying security and the number of outstanding shares must be significant enough to ensure that the price of the security cannot be easily manipulated. Additionally, the listing standards for single stock futures contracts must be as stringent as the requirements in place for listing stock options on the security. The margin requirement for a single stock futures contract is 20% of the value of the underlying security. This offers several advantages over the margin requirements for purchasing the stock outright in a margin account. The margin deposit of 20% is significantly smaller than the 50% required to purchase the stock outright on margin and unlike the margin account, the buyer of the single stock futures contract is not charged interest to hold the position. It is interesting to note that because the margin requirement for a security futures contract is set as a stated 20% of the contact value and not in dollars and cents per share that a fall in the contract price will cause the margin requirement to fall to 20% of the new lower contract price. Therefore an investor who is long a single stock futures contract who receives a margin call will only have to come up with 20% margin of the new lower contract price. This will result in the investor not having to cover the full fall in value of the contract. Conversely, an investor who is short a single stock futures contract would have to maintain 20% of the new higher contract price and would be required to deposit more than the contract's appreciation. Currently an investor may not engage in cross margining of a single stock future position being held in a futures account with a position in the underlying security being held in a securities account. Another way to look at this is that using a single stock future contract to reduce the risk on an underlying security (or vice versa) will not reduce the margin requirement for either position. Should the underlying stock be subject to a stock split the securities futures contract will be adjusted accordingly. If an investor is long a single stock futures contract for 100 shares at 80 and the stock splits 2:1 the investor will now own 2 futures contracts for 100 shares at a price of 40. The value of the shares covered by the contract remains constant both before and after the split. Should the security undergo an odd split such as a 3:2 the price of the contract would be decreased and the number of shares in the contract would increase to 150 shares with the total value remaining unchanged.

 TAKE**NOTE!**

An investor who elects to establish a position in a single stock future, rather than a position in the underlying security is seeking to add alpha (relative out performance) or said to be trying to capture alpha.

FOREIGN CURRENCY FUTURES

International trade requires businesses to purchase and sell goods and services in a variety of different currencies. Many businesses will simply elect to exchange or trade currency in the interbank market or spot market. The interbank market is a vast decentralized, unregulated marketplace where currencies are exchanged. In a spot market transaction the parties agree to exchange two different currencies at whatever the going exchange rate is at that time. Spot market transactions will settle with the delivery of the currencies in 2 business days. Forward contracts are also used in the currency markets by corporations and banks doing business internationally. A forward contract is an agreement to exchange the stated currencies at a time exceeding 2 business days. If a corporation knows that it needs to make a payment for a purchase in foreign currency 3 months from now, the corporation can arrange to purchase the currency from a bank the day before the payment is due. The big drawback with forwards is that there is no secondary market for the contracts.

The value of one currency relative to another constantly fluctuates. The U.S. dollar is the benchmark against which the value of all other currencies is measured. During any given point, one U.S. dollar may buy more or less of another country's currency. Businesses engaged in international trade can hedge their currency risks through the use of foreign currency futures. Foreign currency futures may also be used by investors to speculate on the direction of a currency's value relative to the U.S. dollar.

As the value of another country's currency rises, the value of the U.S. dollar falls. As a result, it would now take more U.S. dollars to purchase one unit of that foreign currency. Conversely, if the value of the foreign currency falls, the value of the U.S. dollar will rise, and it would now take fewer U.S. dollars to purchase one unit of the foreign currency. The values of foreign currencies are inversely related to each other. Foreign currency futures trade on the Chicago Mercantile Exchange. The exchange sets the amount of the foreign currency covered under each contract and the delivery month. Foreign currency futures settle in the exchange or delivery of the currencies.

Businesses and investors will trade foreign currency futures for very different reasons. A business will trade foreign currency futures to manage its foreign currency risk. An importer will purchase foreign currency futures for the currency of the country where it purchases products to reduce the risk of that country's currency rising in value in relation to the U.S. dollar. If the country's currency becomes stronger, it will take more U.S. dollars to purchase the same amount of the foreign currency. As a result, the cost to the importer will rise. Alternatively, in the case of an exporter a fall in the value of a foreign currency relative to the dollar would cause the exporter to realize a lower sales price for their products once the payment in the foreign currency is converted into U.S. dollars. As a result, the exporter, to manage foreign currency risk, will sell futures on the foreign currency.

An investor in foreign currency futures would take the following positions given the following circumstances:

An investor would buy foreign currency futures if:

- There is good economic news from that country.
- The stock market in that country rises.
- There is a large discovery of oil or gold in that country.
- Government instability subsides.

An investor would sell foreign currency futures if:

- There is bad economic news from that country.
- The stock market in that country falls.
- There is an increase in political instability.

The following table details the number of units of foreign currency covered under several of the major foreign currency futures contracts.

Currency	Australian Dollar	British Pound	Canadian Dollar	Euro	Japanese Yen	Swiss Franc
Contract size	100,000	62,500	100,000	125,000	12,500,000	125,000
Minimum price increment	$.0001 per Australian dollar increments ($10.00/contract)	$.0001 per British pound increments ($6.25/contract)	$.0001 per Canadian dollar increments ($10.00/contract)	$.0001 per euro increments ($12.50/contract)	$.000001 per Japanese yen increments ($12.50/contract)	$.0001 per Swiss franc increments ($12.50/contract)

 TAKE**NOTE!**

You will not be required to remember the amount of the foreign currency covered under the contract. If you receive a question relating to foreign currency, the question will contain the amount of the foreign currency covered under the contract. Once you have determined the quoted price of the foreign currency in dollars, multiply it by the number of foreign currency units covered by the contract to determine the contract value.

Pretest

1. Corn futures contracts trading on the CME cover

    a. 10,000 bushels.

    b. 2,500 bushels.

    c. 5,000 bushels.

    d. 50,000 bushels.

2. The minimum price variation per contract is known as a tick and is set by the CFTC.

    True
    False

3. The daily price limits for any given commodity are set by the

    a. NFA.

    b. CFTC.

    c. Board of directors.

    d. Floor officials.

4. If the daily price limit is increased for a given commodity due to extreme volatility, the CBOT and CME will automatically increase the minimum margin required to hold those contracts.

    True
    False

5. The amount of par value covered by a Treasury futures contract is:
   a. 1 bond with $1,000,000 par value.
   b. 10 bonds with $100,000 par value.
   c. 100 bonds with $1,000 par value.
   d. 1 bond with $100,000 par value.

6. A crop year for a commodity covers the time when the commodity is harvested by farmers and runs until:
   a. The first delivery period.
   b. The time the commodity enters an exchange-approved facility.
   c. The next harvest.
   d. The spring planting.

7. The minimum increment change for a T-bill contract in dollar terms is:
   a. $100.
   b. $50.
   c. $10.
   d. $25.

8. The S&P 500 futures contract settles with the delivery of shares of the 500 companies contained in the index, based on the shares weighting in the index.

   True
   False

9. An investor would buy foreign currency futures if all of the following take place in that foreign country EXCEPT:
   a. There is good economic news from that country.
   b. The stock market in that country rises.
   c. There is a large discovery of oil or gold in that country.
   d. The government is replaced by a new regime.

10. An investor who believes that the S&P 500 would decline from 1535 to 1500 enters the following order:

    Sell 1 March S&P 500 at 1535

    The S&P 500 falls to 1510 and the investor offsets his position with a closing purchase. The investor realized:

    a. A gain of $2,500.

    b. A gain of $25,000.

    c. A gain of $6,250.

    d. A gain of $10,000.

Price Forecasting

INTRODUCTION

A large number of factors drive the price of any given futures contract. Chief among these factors is the price of the underlying cash commodity or financial instrument. As the price of the underlying commodity or instrument changes, the price of the futures contract will change. The price of the futures contract has a direct correlation to the price of the underlying commodity or instrument upon which the contract is based. The relationship between the price of the futures contract and the price of the underlying commodity or instrument is kept in a tight range, as the forces of an efficient market continually monitor the relationship. Sophisticated traders and funds are constantly running the prices of the cash and futures markets through advanced pricing models, seeking out opportunities that result from pricing inefficiencies.

FUTURES MARKET PRICING STRUCTURE

The pricing structure of the futures market in relationship to the physical cash commodity in normal market conditions is upward sloping. That is to say that the price of the futures trades above the price of the cash commodity and that futures contracts have successively higher prices the further the delivery date extends. A market that has distant contract months trading at prices higher than near-term contract months is said to be contango, a premium market, a carrying charge market, or a normal market. The price of the cash commodity and near and distant futures contracts will all tend to move in the same direction. If the price of the underlying commodity rises, the price of the near and distant futures contracts will rise. The opposite is true when the price of the underlying commodity falls. As the delivery month approaches, the price of the cash commodity and spot futures contract will converge, effectively pricing the contract during the delivery period as if it was equal to the cash commodity. During normal market conditions the corn market may look as follows:

January 5

Cash Corn	420
March	427
May	436
July	443
September	449
December	456

The corn market in the table above is shown with all delivery months trading at a premium to the cash market. The premium in prices for each successive delivery month is based in part on the carrying charge for the commodity. The carrying charge for a commodity is the total of storage charges, insurance, and any interest paid on borrowed funds.

EXAMPLE

Cash corn on January 5th is trading in the spot market at $4.20 per bushel. If the storage fee for corn is 3 cents per bushel per month and insurance is 1 cent per bushel per month, the total carrying charge for corn is 4 cents per bushel per month. If a user of corn needed to secure corn for use in March (2 months from the date in the table) he could either purchase corn in the cash market and pay the carrying costs or purchase March corn futures and accept delivery of the corn at that time. The price of corn in the cash market is $4.20 per bushel and the carrying cost for corn is 4 cents per bushel per month. The total cost to purchase corn and store it for 2 months would be $4.28 per bushel. With March corn futures trading at $4.27 per bushel it would be cheaper for the user to purchaser March corn futures and accept delivery. This would save the user 1 cent per bushel.

Alternatively, if the market for corn futures exceeds the cost of the commodity plus the carrying charges there would be an opportunity to profit from holding the cash commodity and selling the futures contract against it. Such would be the case if the corn market was priced as follows:

January 5 Normal Market

Cash Corn	420
March	432
May	436
July	443
September	449
December	456

If we use the same carrying charges of 4 cents per month, an investor would be able to lock in a profit with the market structure above by purchasing corn in the cash market and selling the March futures contract. If an investor purchased cash corn at $4.20 per bushel and sold the March contract at $4.32 per bushel. The total cost to purchase and store the corn for 2 months would be $4.28. Having sold the March futures contract against the long cash corn, the investor would have locked in a profit of 4 cents per bushel. During times of supply shortages the market for a given commodity may become inverted where the price of the cash commodity is trading at a premium to the futures contract prices. When this occurs, users of the commodity scramble to acquire the commodity and bid up the prices in the cash market and for the near-term futures contracts to ensure that they will have enough of the commodity to meet their needs. The price of the distant futures contracts is lower than the price of the near-term month contracts as the market prices in new supply and anticipates an end to the shortage. When this pricing structure occurs the market is said to be in backwardation.

January 5 Inverted Market

Cash Corn	470
March	460
May	455
July	450
September	445
December	440

When a market becomes inverted there are no real opportunities to profit from taking delivery of the commodity and selling distant futures contracts, as the price of the cash commodity already exceeds the price of the distant futures contract.

EXAMPLE

If an investor purchases cash corn at 4.70 per bushel in January and sold the March futures contract at $4.60 per bushel, the investor would be locking in a 10-cent loss. When carrying charges are added to the investor's purchase price, the investor's loss would be increased. If we use the carrying charges of 3 cents per bushel for storage and 1 cent per bushel for insurance per month, the total carrying charge for the 2 months would be 8 cents per bushel, the investor's total loss would be 18 cents per bushel

AGRICULTURAL FUTURES PRICING

One of the most influential pricing forces for any given commodity is supply and demand. When the supply of a given commodity is low in relation to the demand for the commodity, the price of that commodity will tend to rise. Alternatively, when the supply of a commodity is abundant in relation to the demand for the commodity, the price of the commodity will tend to fall. The supply of any given commodity is very closely watched by all market participants. Users, producers, and speculators all monitor the amount of the commodity available for delivery as well as the production forecasts for upcoming seasons. The exchanges where the commodities (other than grains) trade publish daily reports of the amount of certified stock available for settlement of futures contracts. For the grain complex, both the Commodity Futures Trading Commission (CFTC) and Chicago Board of Trade (CBOT) report the supply of grains available for delivery. These reports are published weekly and used by the market to forecast future prices. The visible supply report is released each Monday by the CBOT. For grains, the visible supply includes grains that are in storage elevators, are in transit, or are on loading docks. The amount of grain that remains on the farm is not included in the visible supply. Changes to the visible supply can signal upcoming shortages or surpluses for the commodity. As a result, the movement of the commodity through the delivery channel is closely watched. If the visible supply falls it could signal a potential shortage and indicate rising prices. A decrease in the visible supply would be seen as the grain moves out of the elevators and to final users of the commodity. Alternatively, if the visible supply began to increase, it could signal a pending surplus and lower prices. An indication of an increase to the visible supply can be seen as the commodity moves from the farm into storage elevators. As the grain moves off the farm it becomes part of the visible supply. The CFTC also publishes the commitment of traders report each Friday at 3:30 p.m. The report contains the positions of large commercial traders for each commodity with at least 20 large open contract positions. The report can be used to determine the sentiment of the large players in the marketplace. The report shows the large open contract positions as of the prior Tuesday.

SUPPLY AND DEMAND ELASTICITY

The supply and demand for any given commodity may be elastic or inelastic based on changes in the price of the commodity. This is known as price elasticity. If the price of a commodity increases and the demand for the commodity remains the same the demand for the commodity is said to be inelastic. That is because the change in the price of the commodity did not result in a change in the amount of the commodity purchased. Alternatively, if an increase in the price of the commodity resulted in lower demand for the commodity, the demand for that commodity would be said to be elastic. Conversely, if the price of a commodity increased and it attracted new producers, the supply for that commodity would be said to be elastic as the change in price resulted in a change in the supply. If an increase in price did not result in increased supply, the supply would be said to be inelastic. The cost of establishing production or to entering a market will greatly impact the elasticity of the supply for a given commodity. The greater the costs and barriers to entry the more inelastic the supply for the commodity will be. The supply for agricultural products tends to be elastic as farmers adjust production relatively quickly to a change in the price for any given commodity.

GOVERNMENT AGRICULTURAL PROGRAMS

The U.S. government operates several programs that influence the prices of agricultural products. The U.S. government through the use of tariffs, subsidies, and acreage control programs can strongly influence the supply and pricing for certain commodities. When the government levies a tariff on imported commodities it will make those commodities coming from other countries less competitive and as a result will increase demand for the domestically grown products. This should have a stimulative effect on prices for the commodity. Should the government lower the tariff on a given commodity, foreign growers may flood the market with the commodity and drive prices down. Governmental subsidies tend to set a minimum price for the given commodity. These subsidies are designed to help ensure that the producers of the commodities can sell the commodity in the market at a price that is higher than the cost to grow the commodity. Acreage control programs are designed to limit the amount of the commodity that will be grown each year and therefore limit supply. The reduced supply will generally tend to provide support to the price of the commodity in the marketplace. The Government through the use of acreage control programs pays farmers not to produce the commodity on some or all of their available farmland. The U.S. Department of Agriculture operates the Commodity

Credit Corporation or CCC to provide financing to farmers who grow and produce many of the commodities we use every day. Farmers may pledge their harvested and stored crops as collateral for loans. The CCC provides farmers with loans that may be renewed annually for terms of up to 3 years. The sole collateral for the loans are the stored commodities. Should the farmer default on the loan, the CCC has no recourse other than taking possession of the pledged commodity. Liquidation of the commodities by the CCC is strictly regulated. The CCC may not sell the commodity in the open market in any way that would compete with domestic commodity producers. The CCC may only liquidate the forfeited commodity if the commodity is in immediate danger of spoiling.

CROP YEAR

Agricultural contracts are based upon the crop year for the particular commodity. A crop year for a commodity covers the time when the commodity is harvested by farmers and runs until the harvest period of the following year. The harvest period is the time when the commodity has grown to maturity and when farmers who produce the commodity prepare their crops for delivery to market. Because all farmers who produce the commodity are subject to the same growing season for the commodity, the harvest is a time when a tremendous amount of the commodity is released for sale in the marketplace. As a result of the increased supply during the harvest, the price of the commodity tends to be at the lowest price for the crop year. For example, the crop year for corn is September 1 to August 31. This means that farmers all harvest their corn and bring it to market in September of each year. As a result of the harvest in September one would expect corn prices to be at their lowest level during the harvest month of September. In normal markets in this situation one would expect the price of the September corn contract to be lower than the price of the August contract, as the August contract still represents the previous crop year's production. An exception to this rule would be when the forecast for production for the upcoming crop year is below the production of the current crop year and when corn from the current crop year is still abundant in the marketplace. If this condition existed in the corn market, one would expect the September futures contract to be trading at a premium to the August corn contract.

ECONOMIC POLICY

The government has two tools that it can use to try to influence the direction of the economy. Monetary policy, which is controlled by the Federal Reserve

Board, determines the nation's money supply, while fiscal policy is controlled by the president and Congress and determines government spending and taxation.

TOOLS OF THE FEDERAL RESERVE BOARD

The Federal Reserve Board will try to steer the economy through the business cycle by adjusting the level of money supply and interest rates. The Fed may:

- Change the reserve requirement for member banks
- Change the discount rate charged to member banks
- Set target rates for federal fund loans
- Buy and sell U.S. government securities through open-market operations
- Change the amount of money in circulation
- Use moral suasion

INTEREST RATES

Interest rates, put simply, are the cost of money. Overall interest rates are determined by the supply and demand for money, along with any upward price movement in the cost of goods and services, known as inflation. There are several key interest rates upon which all other rates depend:

- Discount rate
- Federal funds rate
- Broker call loan rate
- Prime rate

THE DISCOUNT RATE

The discount rate is the interest rate that the Federal Reserve Bank charges on loans to member banks. A bank may borrow money directly from the Federal Reserve by going to the discount window, and the bank will be charged the discount rate. The bank is then free to lend out this money at a higher rate and earn a profit, or it may use these funds to meet a reserve requirement shortfall. Although a bank may borrow money directly from the Federal Reserve, this is discouraged, and the discount rate has become largely symbolic.

FEDERAL FUNDS RATE

The federal funds rate is the rate that member banks charge each other for overnight loans. The federal funds rate is widely watched as an indicator for the direction of short-term interest rates.

BROKER CALL LOAN RATE

The broker call loan rate is the interest rate that banks charge on loans to broker dealers to finance their customers' margin purchases. Many broker dealers will extend credit to their customers to purchase securities on margin. The broker dealers will obtain the money to lend to their customers from the bank, and the loan is callable or payable on demand by the broker dealer.

PRIME RATE

The prime rate is the rate that banks charge their largest and most creditworthy corporate customers on loans. The prime rate has lost a lot of its significance in recent years because mortgage lenders are now basing their rates on other rates, such as the 10-year Treasury note. The prime rate is, however, very important for consumer spending, because most credit card interest rates are based on prime plus a margin.

RESERVE REQUIREMENT

Member banks must keep a percentage of their depositors' assets in an account with the Federal Reserve. This is known as the reserve requirement. The reserve requirement is intended to ensure that all banks maintain a certain level of liquidity. Banks are in business to earn a profit by lending money. As the bank accepts accounts from depositors, it pays them interest on their money. The bank, in turn, takes the depositors' money and loans it out at higher rates, earning the difference. If the Fed wanted to stimulate the economy, it might reduce the reserve requirement for the banks, which would allow the banks to lend more. By making more money available to borrowers, interest rates will fall and, therefore, demand will increase, helping to stimulate the economy. If the Fed wanted to slow down the economy, it might increase the reserve requirement. The increased requirement would make less money available to borrowers. Interest rates would rise as a result and the demand for goods and services would slow down. Changing the reserve requirement is the least-used Fed tool.

CHANGING THE DISCOUNT RATE

The Federal Reserve Board may change the discount rate in an effort to guide the economy through the business cycle. Remember, the discount rate is the rate that the Fed charges member banks on loans. This rate is highly symbolic, but as the Fed changes the discount rate, all other interest rates change with it. If the Fed wanted to stimulate the economy, it would reduce the discount rate. As the discount rate falls, all other interest rates fall with it, making the cost of money lower. The lower interest rate should encourage borrowing and demand to help stimulate the economy. If the Fed wanted to slow the economy down, it would increase the discount rate. As the discount rate increases, all other rates go up with it, raising the cost of borrowing. As the cost of borrowing increases, demand and the economy slow down.

FEDERAL OPEN MARKET COMMITTEE

The Federal Open Market Committee (FOMC) is the Fed's most flexible tool. The FOMC through open-market operations will buy and sell U.S. government securities in the secondary market in order to control the money supply. If the Fed wants to stimulate the economy and reduce rates, it will buy government securities. When the Fed buys the securities, money is instantly sent into the banking system. As the money flows into the banks, more money is available to lend. Because there is more money available, interest rates will go down and borrowing and demand should increase to stimulate the economy. If the Fed wants to slow the economy down it will sell U.S. government securities. When the Fed sells the securities, money flows from the banks and into the Fed, thus reducing the money supply. Because there is less money available to be loaned out, interest rates will increase, slowing borrowing and demand. This will have a cooling effect on the economy. The FOMC also issues statements that can "jawbone" investors to take certain actions and sets a benchmark for what it believes the fed funds rate should be. However, the marketplace is the ultimate factor in setting the fed funds rate.

MONEY SUPPLY

Prior to determining an appropriate economic policy, economists must have an idea of the amount of money that is in circulation, along with the amount of other types of assets that will provide access to cash. Economists gauge the money supply using three measures. They are:

- M1
- M2
- M3

M1

M1 is the largest and most liquid measure of the nation's money supply and it includes:

- Cash
- Demand deposits (Checking accounts)

M2

Includes all the measures in M1 plus:

- Money market instruments
- Time deposits of less than $100,000
- Negotiable CDs exceeding $100,000
- Overnight repurchase agreements

M3

Includes all of the measures in M1 and M2 plus

- Time deposits greater than $100,000
- Repurchase agreements with maturities greater than 1 day

DISINTERMEDIATION

Disintermediation occurs when people take their money out of low yielding accounts offered by financial intermediaries or banks and invest money in higher yielding investments.

MORAL SUASION

The Federal Reserve Board often will use moral suasion as a way to influence the economy. The Fed is very powerful and very closely watched. By simply implying or expressing their views on the economy, they can slightly influence the economy.

Monetarists believe that a well-managed money supply, with an increasing bias, will produce price stability and will promote the overall economic health of the economy. Milton Friedman is believed to be the founder of the monetarist movement.

FISCAL POLICY

Fiscal policy is controlled by the president and Congress and determines how they manage the budget and government expenditures to help steer the economy through the business cycle. Fiscal policy may change the levels of:

- Federal spending
- Federal taxation
- Creation or use of federal budget deficits or surpluses

Fiscal policy assumes that the government can influence the economy by adjusting its level of spending and taxation. If the government wanted to stimulate the economy, it may increase spending. The assumption here is that as the government spends more, it will increase aggregate demand and, therefore, productivity. Additionally, if the government wanted to stimulate the economy, it may reduce the level of taxation. As the government reduces taxes, it leaves a larger portion of earnings for the consumers and businesses to spend. This should also have a positive impact on aggregate demand. Alternatively, if the government wanted to slow down the economy, it may reduce spending to lower the level of aggregate demand or raise taxes to reduce demand by taking money out of the hands of the consumers. John Maynard Keynes believed that it was the duty of the government to be involved with controlling the direction of the economy and the nation's overall economic health.

As both the Federal Reserve Board and the government monitor the overall health of the U.S. economy, they look at various indicators some of which are:

- Consumer price index
- Inflation/deflation
- Real GDP

CONSUMER PRICE INDEX (CPI)

The consumer price index is made up of a basket of goods and services that consumers most often use in their daily lives. The consumer price index is used to measure the rate of change in overall prices. A CPI that is rising would indicate that prices are going up and that inflation is present. A falling CPI would indicate that prices are falling and deflation is present.

INFLATION/DEFLATION

Inflation is the persistent increase in prices, while deflation is the persistent decrease in prices. Both economic conditions can harm a county's economy. Inflation will eat away at the purchasing power of the dollar and results in higher prices for goods and services. Deflation will erode corporate profits as weak demand in the marketplace drives prices for goods and services lower.

REAL GDP

Real GDP is adjusted for the effects of inflation or deflation over time. GDP is measured in constant dollars so that the gain or loss of the dollar's purchasing power will not show as a change in the overall productivity of the economy.

Both monetary policy and fiscal policy have a major effect on the stock market as a whole.

The following are bullish for the stock market:

- Falling interest rates
- Increasing money supply
- Increase in government spending
- Falling taxes

The following are bearish for the stock market:

- Increasing taxes
- Increasing interest rates
- Falling government spending
- Falling money supply

INTERNATIONAL MONETARY CONSIDERATIONS

The world has become a global marketplace. Each country's economy is affected to some degree by the economies of other countries. Currency values relative to other currencies will impact a country's international trade and the balance of payments. The amount of another country's currency that may be received for a country's domestic currency is known as the exchange rate. The balance of payments measures the net inflow (surplus) or outflow (deficit) of money. The largest component of the balance of payments is the balance of trade. As the exchange rates fluctuate, one country's goods may become more expensive, while another county's goods become less expensive. A weak currency benefits exporters, while a strong currency benefits importers.

LONDON INTERBANK OFFERED RATE / LIBOR

LIBOR is the most widely used measure of short-term interest rates around the world. The LIBOR rate is the market-driven interest rate charged by and between financial institutions, similar to the fed funds rate in the United States. LIBOR loans range from 1 day to 1 year and the rate is calculated by the British Banker's Association in a variety of currencies including euros, U.S. dollars, and yes.

YIELD CURVE ANALYSIS

Economists and investors may analyze both the cost of borrowed funds given various maturities and the general health of the economy by looking at the shape of the yield curve. With a normal, ascending, positive, or upward sloping yield curve, the level of interest rates increases as the term of the maturity increases. Simply put, lenders are going to demand higher interest rates on longer-term loans. The longer the lenders have to wait to be repaid and the longer their money is at risk, the higher the level of compensation (interest) required to make the loan. Higher interest rates also compensate the lenders for the time value of money. The dollars received in 10, 20, or 30 years will be worth less than the value of the dollars loaned to borrowers today. An upward slopping curve is present during times of economic prosperity and depicts the expectation of increased interest rates in the future. The yield curve will also graphically demonstrate investor's expectations about inflation. The higher the expectations are for inflation, the higher the level of corresponding interest rates for the period of high inflation. Occasionally the yield curve may become inverted, negative, or downward sloping during times when demand for short-term funds are running much higher than the demand for longer-term loans or in times where the Federal Reserve Board has increased short-term rates to combat an economy that is growing too quickly and threatening long-term price stability. With an inverted yield curve, interest rates on short-term loans far exceed the interest rates on longer-term loans. An inverted yield curve tends to normalize quickly and is often a precursor to a recession. The yield curve may also flatten out when the interest rates for both short-term and long-term loans are approximately equal to one another.

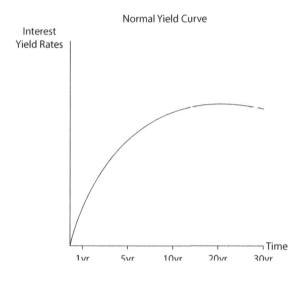

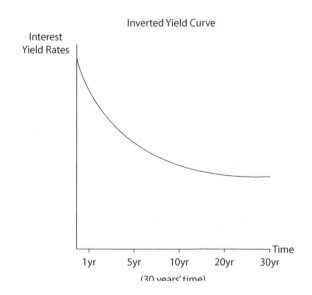

TECHNICAL ANALYSIS

A technical analyst uses the patterns created by the past price performance of the commodity to predict the direction of the commodity price in the future. A technical analyst is not concerned with the fundamentals of the market or even how the commodity is used. They are only interpreting chart patterns and other technical factors relating to the price performance of the commodity. Some of the chart patterns that a technical analyst will look to identify are:

- Support
- Resistance
- Trendlines
- Reversals
- Consolidations

Support: Support is created at the point to which the commodity falls and attracts buyers. The new buyers that are brought into the market because of the lower price create demand for the commodity and prevent it from falling any further.

Resistance: Resistance is created at the point to which the commodity appreciates and attracts sellers. The new sellers that are brought into the market because of the higher price create supply for the commodity and prevent it from rising any further.

Upward trendlines: An upward trendline is characterized by a series of higher highs and a series of higher lows. A chartist would draw a line connecting the series of higher lows to confirm the trend, and the trendline should provide some support to the commodity price.

Downward trendlines: A downward trendline is characterized by a series of lower highs and a series of lower lows. A chartist would draw a line connecting the series of lower highs to confirm the downward trend, and the trendline should provide some resistance to the commodity price.

Reversals: A reversal indicates a significant change in the price action of the commodity. A bullish reversal indicates the end of a downward trend and the beginning of a new upward trend. A bearish reversal indicates the end of an upward trend and the beginning of a new downward trend. One of the most significant reversal patterns is the head and shoulders formation. A head and shoulders top is a bearish reversal of an up trend, while a head and shoulders bottom is a bullish reversal of a downtrend.

Consolidation: A consolidation pattern is characterized by a horizontal movement in the commodity price. Buyers and sellers are attracted to the market and are willing to trade the commodity at almost the same prices.

The following illustrate the chart patterns outlined above:

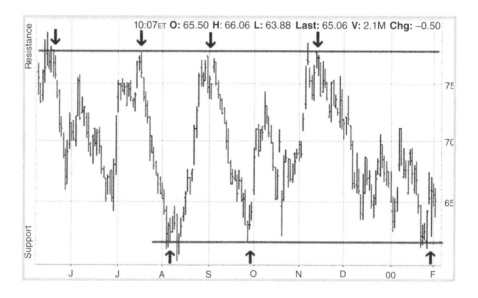

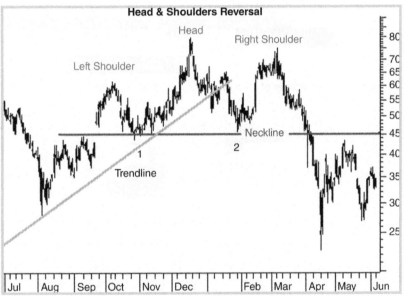

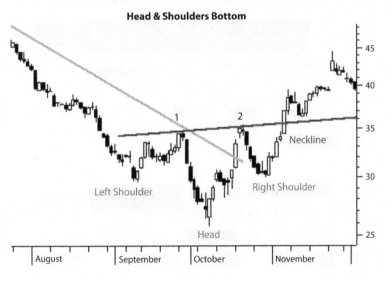

OPEN INTEREST

Open interest is also a very important indicator to watch for signs of the market's strength and direction. The open interest in a futures contract is the total number of contracts outstanding that have not yet been closed or offset. Because all futures are two-party contracts, for every long position there must be a corresponding short position. The amount of open interest is determined as follows:

EXAMPLE

A new contract month has just started trading in gold futures and as a result there is no open interest. A customer of merchant A who thinks gold is going to rise buys one of the newly listed gold contracts from a customer of merchant B who thinks that the price is likely to fall. The new gold contract now has total open interest of one contract.

Customer of merchant A	Long 1 new gold contract	
Customer of merchant B		Short 1 new gold contract
Total open interest in new gold contract		1 contract

A customer of Merchant C now buys 10 new gold contracts from a customer of Merchant D. Open interest would now be as follows:

Customer of merchant A	Long 1 new gold contract	
Customer of merchant B		Short 1 new gold contract
Customer of merchant C	Long 10 new gold contracts	
Customer of merchant D		Short 10 new gold contracts
Total open interest in new gold contract		11 contracts

Now if the gold market rallies and the customer of merchant C decides to sell 5 new gold contracts and take a profit on half of his position by selling 5 contracts to a pit trader, the open interest would look as follows:

Customer of merchant A	Long 1 new gold contract	
Customer of merchant B		Short 1 new gold contract
Customer of merchant C	Long 5 new gold contracts	
Customer of merchant D		Short 10 new gold contracts
Pit trader	Long 5 new gold contracts	
Total open interest in new gold contract		11 contracts

Notice how the total open interest did not change because the pit trader came into the market and established a new long position that was being offset by a previous long.

Finally, as the market makes a move higher, the pit trader sells the 5 contracts to the customer of Merchant D who is looking to close out the unprofitable short position.

Customer of merchant A	Long 1 new gold contract	
Customer of merchant B		Short 1 new gold contract
Customer of merchant C	Long 5 new gold contracts	
Customer of merchant D		Short 5 new gold contracts
Pit trader	Flat and has exited the market	
Total open interest in new gold contract		6 contracts

Because the pit trader offset his long position by selling his 5 contracts to the customer of merchant D who was looking to offset his short position, the total open interest has been reduced by 5 contracts.

 TAKENOTE!

To determine open interest you never add open long and open short positions. Each open futures contract consists of 1 open long position and 1 open short position.

The higher the open interest is in a contract, the higher the liquidity will be in that contract. This is because there are more parties interested in trading the contract. An increase in open interest and liquidity will also lead to smaller spreads between the bids and offers for the contract.

As open interest increases in a futures contract, it is an indication that new positions are being established as market participants enter the market. Alternatively, as open interest decreases, it is an indication that market participants are exiting the market. Changes in open interest can confirm or contradict trends in the market and can be used by technical analysts as a price-forecasting tool to help determine when to establish or exit a position.

The following table shows how an analyst would look at the market given various price action associated with changes in open interest.

Direction of Open Interest	Direction of Market Prices	Technical Consideration	Take Away
Open interest increasing	Price of commodity rising	Technically strong market	New buyers and sellers are entering the market establishing new positions and the buyers are more aggressive, driving prices higher
Open interest increasing	Price of commodity falling	Technically weak market	New buyers and sellers are entering the market establishing new positions and the sellers are more aggressive, driving prices lower
Open interest falling	Price of commodity falling	Technically strong market	Long positions are being liquidated faster than new positions are being established. Longs are selling more positions than shorts are establishing. This is known as a liquidating market.
Open interest falling	Price of commodity increasing	Technically weak market	Short positions are being covered faster than new positions are being established. Shorts are covering more positions than new longs are establishing. The shorts are exiting the market driving prices higher. Once most of the shorts have covered, prices will tend to reverse.

Pretest

1. A market that has distant contract months trading at prices higher than near-term contract months is said to be:

   a. Inverted.

   b. Expensive.

   c. Contango.

   d. Sloping.

2. As the delivery month approaches, the price of the cash commodity and spot futures contract will converge.

   True

   False

3. The premium in prices for each successive delivery month is based in part on:

   a. The fact that demand is always increasing for agricultural commodities.

   b. The fact that distant months always trade higher than near-term contracts.

   c. The carrying charges for the commodity.

   d. The higher cost to clear distant month contracts.

4. All of the following make up the carrying charges for a cash commodity EXCEPT:

   a. Margin interest.

   b. Insurance.

   c. Storage fees.

   d. Interest on borrowed funds.

5. A large bread baking company knows that it will need 50,000 bushels of wheat in 3 months. The cost of wheat in the spot market is 5.50 per bushel. Carrying charges for wheat are 4 cents per bushel for storage and 1.5 cents per bushel for insurance. The price of the wheat futures contract 3 months out is 5.65 per bushel. The company in this case is better off buying wheat in the cash market now and storing it.

   True

   False

6. During times of supply shortages the market for a given commodity may become_____, where the price of the cash commodity is trading at a premium to the futures contract prices.

   a. Contango

   b. Convex

   c. Forwarded

   d. Inverted

7. For the grain complex, both the CFTC and CBOT report the supply of grains available for delivery. These reports are published

   a. Daily.

   b. Weekly.

   c. Monthly.

   d. During each delivery period.

8. Resistance is created at the point to which the commodity falls and attracts buyers. The new buyers that are brought into the market support the price of the commodity.

   True

   False

9. The higher the open interest is in a contract, the higher

   a. The price.

   b. The liquidity.

   c. The margin requirement.

   d. The volatility.

10. The market for a particular commodity is seeing a general increase in open interest while prices are trending higher. This type of market is known as a technically:

   a. Weak market.

   b. Strong market.

   c. Liquid market.

   d. Trendless market.

Speculation and Hedging

INTRODUCTION

The two main types of participants in the futures markets are the speculators and the hedgers. The objective of the speculator is to make a profit based on their belief about the future price action of a commodity. Speculators come in all shapes and sizes, from the very large and sophisticated to the individual investor who wants to make money trading the futures market. Large funds, pit traders, and individual investors all seek to profit by deploying risk capital in the futures market and take on the risk that hedgers are seeking to eliminate. The objective of the hedger is to reduce risk. Hedgers are not trying to make a profit on the futures contracts, they are seeking to reduce the risk of losses by using futures contracts. Hedgers are largely made up of users and producers of the commodities. Users of the commodities are concerned that prices of the commodities needed to operate their businesses may increase and result in lower profits or even cause the user to suffer losses. Commodity producers are seeking to sell their products at the highest possible price and are concerned that falling prices will cause their profits to fall or even cause them to suffer losses.

SPECULATION

The motive of a speculator is to realize a profit on a position in a futures contract based on change in the value of the futures contract. A speculator will buy or take a long futures position when they expect the value of the commodity to increase.

EXAMPLE   A trader who speculates on the price of crude oil reads an article about the political unrest in the Middle East that could cause a disruption in the shipment of crude oil from the region. Should the shipment of crude from the Middle East fall, supply will be reduced until the shipping channels reopen. Believing that the price of crude will increase significantly if the supply is disrupted, the trader decides to purchase crude oil by placing the following order:

Buy 5 December crude at 89

Should the political unrest in the Middle East result in a closure of the shipping lanes and cause crude oil to rise, the investor would realize a profit on his long crude oil contracts.

An investor or speculator who feels that the price of the commodity is likely to decline would establish a short futures position in an effort to profit from the falling commodity price.

EXAMPLE   A trader is reading an article on how the Federal Reserve is seeking to reduce the level of monetary accommodation by lowering the level of its bond purchases. The trader feels that when the level of monetary stimulus is reduced, the value of the dollar will strengthen as a result. The trader believes that a stronger dollar as a result of the Federal Reserve's actions will cause the price of gold to fall. To profit from the anticipated fall in gold prices, the trader enters the following order:

Sell 2 October gold at 1445

Should the price of gold fall as a result of the stronger dollar, the investor would realize a profit on the short gold contracts.

To determine the profit or loss on a speculative futures position one must look at all of the following:

- The number of units per contract
- The price per unit per contract
- The price at which the contract was opened
- The price at which the position was offset or closed
- The number of contracts
- Commissions rates per round-turn contract

Going back to our crude speculator who went long 5 December crude oil contracts at 89, if the price of crude oil for December delivery increased to

92.20 as a result of the political unrest and the trader closes out the position with an offsetting sale of the 5 crude contracts at 92.20, the profit would be calculated as follows:

> **Bought 5 December crude oil at 89**
>
> **Sold 5 December crude oil at 92.20**
>
> **Profit of 3.20 per barrel**

Each crude oil contract represents 1,000 barrels of oil; as a result the profit per contract is $3,200 ($3.20 per barrel × 1,000 barrels). The trader purchased 5 contracts for a total profit of $16,000 ($3,200 per contract × 5 contracts), excluding commissions. If the futures commission merchant (FCM) charges the customer a $50 round-turn commission per contract, the net profit would be $3,150 per contract ($3,200 − 50) and the total net profit would be $15,750 ($3,150 per contract × 5 contracts).

Alternatively, if the price of crude oil for December delivery fell from 89 to 87.5 as supply remained strong and the trader closes out the position with an offsetting sale of the 5 crude contracts at 87.50, the loss would be calculated as follows:

> **Bought 5 December crude oil at 89**
>
> **Sold 5 December crude oil at 87.50**
>
> **Loss of 1.50 per barrel**

Each crude oil contract represents 1,000 barrels of oil, as a result the loss per contract is $1,500 ($1.50 per barrel × 1,000 barrels). The trader purchased 5 contracts for a total loss of $7,500 ($1,500 per contract × 5 contracts), excluding commissions. When factoring in commissions on a losing trade, the commission costs will increase the investor's loss. In this case using the same $50 per round-turn contract commission rate, the loss is increased from $1,500 per contract to $1,550 per contract and the total net loss would be $7,750 ($1,550 × 5 contracts).

Going back to our gold speculator who went short 2 October gold contracts at 1445, if the price of gold fell to 1436.50 as a result of the stronger dollar and the trader closes out the position with an offsetting purchase of 2 October gold contracts at 1436.50, the profit would be calculated as follows:

> **Sold 2 October gold 1445**
>
> **Bought 2 October gold at 1436.50**
>
> **Profit $8.5 per troy ounce**

Each gold contract represents 100 troy ounces. As a result, the profit per contact is $850 ($8.50 × 100 ounces). The trader sold 2 contracts for a total profit of $1,700, excluding commissions. Using the same $50 per round-turn contract commission rate, the total net profit would be $800 per contract or $1,600 total ($800 per contract × 2 contracts).

Alternatively, if the price of gold rose to $1,457 per ounce due to continued weakness in the dollar and the trader closes out the position with an offsetting purchase of 2 October gold contracts at 1457. The loss would be calculated as follows:

Sold 2 October gold 1445

Bought 2 October gold at 1457

Loss of $12 per troy ounce

Each gold contract represents 100 troy ounces. As a result the loss per contact is $1,200 ($12 × 100 ounces). The trader sold 2 contracts for a total loss of $2,400, excluding commissions. Using the same $50 per round-turn contract commission rate, the total loss would be $1,250 per contract or $2,500 total ($1,250 per contract × 2 contracts).

MARGIN

Initial margin is the amount of money that must be deposited to establish a futures position. All margin deposits must be met by the opening of the next business day. The amount is set by the board of directors of the exchange on which the contract trades and the amount is the same for both long and short contract positions. Most FCMs enact "house rules" that require customers to meet higher margin requirements than those set by the exchange. FCMs may never enact rules that set lower margin requirements. The initial margin is effectively a good faith deposit, as most futures positions do not result in making or accepting delivery of the underlying commodity. It is important to remember that both parties to a futures contract are contingently liable for the full value of the futures contract based on the value of the underlying commodity. Unlike a margin account used by customers for the purchase of securities, there is no loan made to the customer who purchases commodities. Futures commission merchants do not loan money to their clients who wish to trade futures contracts and as a result there is no debit balance and no interest changed to the customer. The initial margin requirement is based on a percentage of the total contract value and varies from contract to contract. All futures contracts must be purchased and sold in a margin account. If a customer maintains a securities account and a futures account at the same firm, the customer must sign a transfer or supplement agreement which allows the firm to automatically transfer funds from the client's securities account to the futures account. If the client does not sign this agreement, all transfers must be approved individually in writing. Once the initial margin has been deposited by the customer, the futures commission merchant will monitor the price of the futures contract to ensure that the customer's margin balance does not fall below the minimum maintenance level. This is known as marking to the market. As the price of the futures contract changes in the market, the margin balance in the customer's account will change accordingly. A customer who has purchased the futures contract will see their margin balance (equity) rise when the price of the contract increases and will see their margin balance fall when the price of the contract declines. Conversely a customer who has established a short position in a futures contract will see their margin balance fall as the price of the futures contract increases and will see their margin balance increase as the price of the contract declines.

EXAMPLE   If the initial margin requirement for crude oil is $3.74 per barrel or $3,740 per contract ($3.74 × 1,000 barrels), our crude oil trader who purchased 5 December crude oil at 89 had to deposit the initial margin of $3,740 for each of the 5 contracts. The trader's total required deposit was $18,700. If the price of crude oil for December delivery increased to 92.20 as a result of the political unrest and the trader closes out the position with an offsetting sale of the 5 crude contracts at 92.20, the trader's margin (equity) would have increased from $18,700 (original margin) to $34,700. The margin in the trader's account had increased by $16,000, excluding commissions. The trader made $3.20 per barrel on 5,000 barrels of oil (five 1,000-barrel contracts). This is a return of 85.5% (a $16,000 return on a $18,700 investment).

Alternatively, if the price of crude oil for December delivery fell from 89 to 87.5 as supply remained strong and the trader closes out the position with an offsetting sale of the 5 crude contracts at 87.50, the loss would be calculated as follows:

Bought 5 December crude oil at 89

Sold 5 December crude oil at 87.50

Loss of 1.50 per barrel

In this case the investor lost $1.50 per barrel or $1,500 per contract ($1.50 × 1,000 barrels). Since the investor purchased 5 crude oil contracts, the investor lost a total of $7,500 (5 contracts × $1,500 per contract). The trader's margin (equity) would have fallen from $18,700 (original margin) to $11,200. The trader in this case lost 40% (a $7,500 loss on a $18,700 investment).

Let's go back to our gold speculator who went short 2 October gold contracts. If the initial margin requirement for gold is $79.75 per ounce or $7,975 per contract ($79.75 × 100 troy ounces), our gold trader who sold 2 October gold contracts at 1,445 had to deposit the initial margin of $7,975 for each of the 2 contracts. The trader's total required deposit was $15,950. If the price of gold for October delivery fell to 1436.50 as a result of the stronger dollar and the trader closes out the position with an offsetting purchase of 2 October gold contracts at 1436.50, the trader's margin (equity) would have increased from $15,950 (original margin) to $17,650. The profit is calculated as follows:

Sold 2 October gold 1445

Bought 2 October gold at 1436.50

Profit $8.5 per troy ounce

Each gold contract represents 100 troy ounces. As a result, the profit per contract is $850 ($8.50 × 100 ounces). The trader sold 2 contracts for a total profit of $1,700, excluding commissions. The return on the short gold contracts would be 10.6% (a $1,700 profit on a $15,950 investment).

Alternatively, if the price of gold rose to $1,457 per ounce because the dollar remained weak and the trader closes out the position with an offsetting purchase of 2 October gold contracts at 1457, the loss would be calculated as follows:

Sold 2 October gold 1445

Bought 2 October gold at 1457

Loss of $12 per troy ounce

Each gold contract represents 100 troy ounces. As a result, the loss per contract is $1,200 ($12 × 100 ounces). The trader sold 2 contracts for a total loss of $2,400, excluding commissions. The trader lost 15.04% (a $2,400 loss on a $15,950 investment).

 TAKE**NOTE!**

Because a hedger is reducing risk and not taking it on, the margin requirements for a hedger are often lower than the margin requirements for a speculator.

MAINTENANCE MARGIN

Once an investor establishes a position in a futures contract and deposits the initial margin, the futures commission merchant will monitor changes in the account equity based on the changes to the price of the futures contract (marking to the market). Initial margin is the amount of money that must be deposited to establish a futures position. The amount is set by the board of directors of the exchange on which the contract trades, and the amount is the same for both long and short contract positions. The minimum maintenance is the amount of equity or margin that must be available in the account to maintain an open contract position. The amount of the maintained margin that must be maintained in the account is also set by the board of directors of the exchange on which the contract trades.

OPEN TRADE EQUITY

The open trade equity (OTE) is calculated based on the initial margin deposit plus or minus any unrealized profit or loss on the open contract position. Adverse price moves will cause the customer's OTE or margin balance to fall. Maintenance margin is the minimum equity that a customer must maintain to hold the open futures position. If the customer's equity falls below the minimum maintenance level, the customer will get a call for additional or variance margin. Once the equity in the account falls below the maintenance margin level the customer will be required to deposit enough margin to restore the account to the initial margin requirement. A customer who receives a call for additional margin may meet the call by depositing additional funds from a bank, by transferring funds from another account, or by liquidating futures contracts to restore the required equity. In addition to marking to the market it is important to monitor the customer's account balance and total equity to determine the status of the customer's account. A customer's account balance is the total amount of deposits minus any withdrawals. The customer's total equity is found using the following formula:

total equity = account balance +/ – open trade equity

Let's look at the ledger for our oil trader who purchased 5 December crude oil contracts at 89 and see what happens to his account when the contracts are marked to the market at 92.20 at the close the day before he sold them.

Entry	Deposit or Withdrawal of Funds	Account Balance	OTE	Total Equity
Bought 5 December crude	$18,700	$18,700	–	$18,700
December crude mark to market 92.20		$18,700	$16,000	$34,700

Because the contracts appreciated by $16,000, the customer's OTE was $16,000. The total equity in the account also increased by $16,000 from $18,700 to $34,700. The customer could withdraw the amount by which the equity in the account exceeds the initial requirement (excess equity) or use it to establish other positions. If the customer used the excess equity to purchase additional crude oil contracts thinking that crude was going to continue higher, the trader would be employing a strategy known as pyramiding.

Now let's look at the customer's ledger balance when crude oil falls from 89 to 87.50.

Entry	Deposit or Withdrawal of Funds	Account Balance	OTE	Total Equity
Bought 5 December crude	$18,700	$18,700	–	$18,700
December crude mark to market 87.50		$18,700	($7,500)	$11,200

Because the value contracts fell by $7,500, the customer's OTE was ($7,500). The total equity in the account as a result fell by $7,500 from $18,700 to $11,200. If the minimum maintenance for crude oil is $3.40 per barrel or $3,400 per contract, the trader is going to get a call to deposit additional funds or variation margin to return the account equity to the initial margin requirement as follows:

Entry	Deposit or Withdrawal of Funds	Account Balance	OTE	Total Equity
Bought 5 December crude	$18,700	$18,700	–	$18,700
December crude mark to market 87.50		$18,700	($7,500)	$11,200
Maintenance call $7,500		$18,700	($7,500)	$11,200
Deposit	$7,500	$26,200	($7,500)	$18,700

In this case the equity or margin in the account fell from $3.74 per barrel or $3,740 per contract to $2.24 per barrel or $2,240 per contract. This is well below the minimum maintenance of $3.40 per barrel or $3,400 per contract. As a result, the customer had to deposit the entire amount of the loss or $7,500 to restore the account to its original margin requirement of $18,700. No withdrawals may be made from an under margined account. If the customer wanted to establish new positions in an under margined account, the order may be accepted so long as the FCM has reason to believe that the customer will send in the required margin for the new position along with the funds to meet the margin call.

Let's look at the ledger for our gold trader who sold 2 October gold contracts at 1445 and see what happens to his account when the contracts are marked to the market at 1436.50 at the close the day before he bought them back to close out the position.

Entry	Deposit or Withdrawal of Funds	Account Balance	OTE	Total Equity
Sold 2 October gold	$15,950	$15,950	–	$15,950
October gold mark to market 1436.50		$15,950	$1,700	$17,650

Because the contracts fell in value by $1,700, the customer's OTE was $1,700. The OTE is positive because the customer established a short position. The total equity in the account also increased by $1,700 from $15,950 to $17,650. The customer could withdraw the amount by which the equity in the account exceeds the initial requirement (excess equity) or use it to establish other positions.

Now let's look at the customer's ledger balance when gold rallies against him from 1445 to 1457.

Entry	Deposit or Withdrawal of Funds	Account Balance	OTE	Total Equity
Sold 2 October gold	$15,950	$15,950	–	$15,950
October gold mark to market 1457		$15,950	($2,400)	$13,550

Because the contracts appreciated by $2,400, the customer's OTE was ($2,400). The total equity in the account also fell by $2,400 from $15,950 to $13,550. If the minimum maintenance for gold is $71.50 per ounce or $7,150 per contract, the trader is going to get a call to deposit additional funds or variation margin to return the account equity to the initial margin requirement. The ledger would now look as follows:

Entry	Deposit or Withdrawal of Funds	Account Balance	OTE	Total Equity
Sold 2 October gold	$15,950	$15,950	–	$15,950
October gold mark to market 1457		$15,950	($2,400)	$13,550
Maintenance call $2,400				
Deposit	$2,400	$18,350	($2,400)	$15,950

In this case the equity or margin in the account fell from $79.75 per ounce or $7,975 per contract to $67.75 per ounce or $6,775 per contract. This is well below the minimum maintenance of $71.50 per ounce or $7,150 per contract. As a result, the customer had to deposit the entire amount of the loss or $2,400 to restore the account to its original margin requirement of $15,950. No withdrawals may be made from an under margined account. If the customer wanted to establish a new position in an under margined account, the order may be accepted so long as the FCM has reason to believe that the customer will send in the required margin for the new position along with the funds to meet the margin call.

CHANGES TO THE MARGIN REQUIREMENT

The exchanges establish the initial and minimum maintenance margin based on a measure of value at risk (VAR) and in relation to historical and implied volatility calculations. The greater the value at risk and the higher the level of volatility, the higher the initial and maintenance requirements will be. The initial margin requirement is typically 110% to 135% of the maintenance margin requirement. During times of heightened volatility, the exchanges can increase both the initial and maintenance requirement. The increase will affect investors who want to establish new positions as well as those who have open contract positions. Once the margin requirement is increased, new positions will have to meet the increased initial margin requirements. Open positions that were established under the lower initial margin requirement will not have to deposit funds so long as the equity in the account remains above the higher minimum margin requirement now in force. A customer whose account is impacted by an increased minimum margin who does not deposit more funds may have his / her contracts liquidated by the FCM.

EXAMPLE

An investor who thinks that the price of corn is likely to increase purchases 5 May corn contracts at 5.10.

Each corn contract covers 5,000 bushels of corn. The initial margin requirement is 60 cents per bushel and the maintenance for the contract is 45 cents per bushel. The price of corn spikes to 5.35 and rolls over to close at 5.00 during a particularly volatile trading session. The investor's ledger would not look as follows:

Entry	Deposit or Withdrawal of Funds	Account Balance	OTE	Total Equity
Bought 5 May corn	$15,000	$15,000	–	$15,000

Entry	Deposit or Withdrawal of Funds	Account Balance	OTE	Total Equity
May corn mark to market 5.00		$15,000	($2,500)	$12,500
No call due				

The customer has suffered an unrealized loss but has maintained equity of 50 cents per bushel, which is over the current contract requirement of 45 cents per bushel.

As a result of the volatility in corn, the exchange increases both the initial and maintenance requirements for corn. The exchange increases the initial requirement to 67.5 cents per bushel and the maintenance requirement is increased to 50 cents per bushel. At this point the corn trader still does not have to deposit more funds because his equity is still equal to the higher minimum requirement. If corn fell from 5.00 to 4.98, the ledger would look as follows:

Entry	Deposit or Withdrawal of Funds	Account Balance	OTE	Total Equity
Bought 5 May corn	$15,000	$15,000	–	$15,000
May corn mark to market 5.00		$15,000	($2,500)	$12,500
No call due				
May corn mark to market 4.98		$15,000	($3,000)	$12,000
Maintenance call issued $4,875	$4,875	$19,875	($3,000)	$16,875

As the price of corn continued to drop, the investor's account fell below the new higher maintenance requirement. When that happened a call for additional funds was issued and required the investor to meet the new higher initial margin of 67.5 cents per bushel, resulting in a call for $4,875. The new initial requirement is $3,375 per contract or $16,875 for the 5 contracts. The equity in the account had fallen to $12,000 as the price of corn fell. The call was for the difference between the new initial requirement of $16,875 and the $12,000 in equity or $4,875

OTHER FORMS OF MARGIN DEPOSITS

Some FCMs will allow a customer to meet a margin deposit in forms other than in cash. For example an investor may maintain a letter of credit from a bank with the FCM. An investor may also deposit Treasury bills, notes or bonds as well as stocks, ETFs and corporate bonds. These alternative margin deposits will not have the entire market value of the security credited toward meeting the margin requirement. Stocks and ETFs will be subject to a haircut of 30%. If a customer were to deposit $100,000 of fully paid for stock, the FCM would value that at $70,000 for margin purposes. While gold and corporate bonds will be subject to a 15% and 20% haircut on the market value respectively. The following table shows the haircut applied to various Treasury and agency securities for margin purposes.

Asset Class	0 to ≤1 years	>1 to ≤3 years	>3 to ≤5 years	>5 to ≤10 years	>10 to ≤30 years	>30 years
U.S. Treasury Bills	0.5%	–	–	–	–	–
U.S. Treasury Floating Rate Notes	1%	2%	–	–	–	–
U.S. Treasury Notes	1%	2%	3%	4.5%	6%	–
U.S. Treasury Bonds	1%	2%	3%	4.5%	6%	

Haircut Schedule

Asset Class	Time to Maturity					
	0 to ≤1 years	>1 to ≤3 years	>3 to ≤5 years	>5 to ≤10 years	>10 to ≤30 years	>30 years
Discount Notes and Bills: FFCB, FHLB, FHLMC, FNMA	3.5%	–	–	–	–	–
Coupon Bearing instruments: GSEOTH	4%			5.5%	7%	–

Haircut Schedule

Asset Class	Time to Maturity					
	0 to ≤1 years	>1 to ≤3 years	>3 to ≤5 years	>5 to ≤10 years	>10 to ≤30 years	>30 years
Select nominal Sovereign discount bills from Australia, Canada, France, Germany, Japan, Mexico, Singapore, Sweden, and the United Kingdom	5%			–	–	–

	Time to Maturity					
Asset Class	0 to ≤1 years	>1 to ≤3 years	>3 to ≤5 years	>5 to ≤10 years	>10 to ≤30 years	>30 years
Select fixed-rate, nominal Sovereign notes and bonds from Australia, Canada, France, Germany, Japan, Mexico, Singapore, Sweden, and the United Kingdom	6%			7.5%	9%	10.5%

Take note a letter of credit will not be subject to a haircut and the full amount of the letter will be available for margin purposes.

HEDGING

As we have already discussed, hedgers are always the users or producers of a commodity who are seeking to reduce or eliminate business risk that can result from an adverse change in the price of the commodity. The hedger is not seeking to profit outright from a position in a futures contract. Any profit on the futures contract will be used to offset the negative impact of an adverse price movement in the underlying commodity. Hedgers take futures positions that are opposite to their position in the underlying cash commodity. There are two types of hedgers, long hedgers and short hedgers. The type of hedger gets their name from the position that they take in the futures market to hedge their risk in the cash market. A long hedger will purchase futures to protect from the risk of the price of the commodity going up. A long hedger is someone who uses the commodity or who is contractually obligated to deliver the cash commodity but who does not own the cash commodity. If a business has a need for or an obligation to deliver the physical commodity, they are considered to be short the cash commodity or short the *basis*. Any increase in the price of the cash commodity will have a negative impact on their business, will reduce their profits, or may cause the business to suffer a loss.

CASE STUDY: LONG HEDGER

A large jewelry company knows that it will need a substantial amount of gold to produce the class rings that are ordered in the spring of each year. Competition for the class-ring contracts is significant and as a result pricing power is limited. The company fears that if the price of gold increases it will not be able to pass along the increased gold price to the buyers of the rings. In October gold is selling in the spot market at 1,425 per troy ounce and the company knows it will need 5,000 troy ounces to fill the orders it traditionally receives in April. To meet its demand for gold in April the company may elect to purchase the 5,000 ounces in the spot market and accept delivery. This would require the company to lay out a tremendous amount of cash and pay for storage and insurance of the commodity for the next 6 months. If the company did not have sufficient cash to pay for the gold in full and used a credit facility to finance the purchase, the company's cost would be increased further by paying interest on the borrowed funds. The company also may elect to take no action at this time. This however will leave the company exposed to increased prices and losses should the price of gold rally in the next 6 months. Alternatively and perhaps the best choice is for the jewelry company to purchase gold futures for April delivery. The jewelry company can hedge their need for 5,000 ounces of gold by purchasing 50 April gold contracts. Since each gold contract is for 100 troy ounces, the company has completely hedged their need for gold and is now in a position to accept delivery at the time they begin to receive orders. If spot gold in October is selling at 1425 and the April gold contract is selling for 1435, the company has locked in their delivery price for April at 1435 and can accept delivery to meet its demand.

This is a perfect hedge: the number of units needed and the delivery month meets the need of the user. Let's look at the same scenario, except the need for the gold is in March and the company hedges the price of gold in October with April gold futures

Time	Gold Cash/Spot Price	April Gold Futures Price
October	1425	1435
March	1440	1447.50
Change	+15 (increased cost)	+12.50 (profit on long futures)

In March, the price of spot gold has increased $15 from $1,425 to $1,440 per ounce. During the same time the price of the April gold futures contract has increased from $1,435 to $1,447.50, an increase of $12.50. The jewelry company will now purchase 5,000 ounces of gold in the spot market at $1,440 and will offset the hedge by selling 50 April gold contracts at $1,447.50. In this case the company hedged $12.50 of the $15 price increase in gold. As a result of the hedge the company's effective cost for the 5,000 ounces of gold is $1,427.50 per ounce. The effective cost of $1,427.50 is found as follows: price of spot gold in March $1440 − $12.50 profit on the futures contract equals $1,427.50.

A short hedger will sell futures to protect from the risk of the price of the commodity falling. A short hedger is someone who produces the commodity or who owns the cash commodity. If a business produces the commodity or owns the physical commodity, they are considered to be long the cash commodity or long the *basis*. Any fall in the price of the cash commodity will have a negative impact on their business, will reduce their profits, or may cause the business to suffer a loss.

CASE STUDY: SHORT HEDGER

A farmer in Iowa is operating a third-generation family farm. The main crop for the farm over the last 30 years is corn. With demand for corn strong and prices at historically high levels, the farmer decides to plant substantially more corn this crop year. In April the farmer plants an additional 100 acres of corn, increasing his production by 25% to 500 total acres. As a result of the increased production the farmer is taking on significantly higher expenses in the form of seed, watering, and fertilization costs. The farmer is concerned that the price of corn may fall between the planting season in April and the time when the corn is harvested in mid-September as corn farmers ramp up production to take advantage of the historically high corn price. Due to the unusually high demand forecast, the September futures contract is trading at a premium to cash corn in April, which is trading at 5.10 per bushel, and September corn futures are trading at 5.40. The farmer expects to grow 150 bushels per acre for a total of 75,000 bushels of corn (500 acres × 150 bushels per acre). To hedge his crop production the farmer sells 15 September corn futures contracts at 5.40. Since each corn contract represents 5,000 bushels of corn, the farmer has hedged his entire crop production. When the farmer harvests his crop in September he will deliver the crop production of 75,000 bushels of corn against his 15 short futures contracts and will have locked in the sale price of $5.40 per bushel. This is another example of a perfect hedge. The number of units and the contract delivery month coincided perfectly with the harvest period and with the size of the crop production. Let's look at the same scenario, except let's now place the farmer in part of Iowa where the crop is harvested later, in mid-October. With no corn contracts trading in April for October delivery the farmer must sell December futures contracts to hedge his October crop production and delivery. With cash corn trading at 5.10 and corn futures for December delivery trading at 5.50, the farmer sells 15 December corn futures contracts at 5.50.

Time	Corn Cash/Spot Price	December Corn Futures Price
April	5.10	5.50
October	4.90	5.32
Change	−0.20 (loss on commodity)	−0.18 (profit on short futures)

In October the price of spot corn has fallen by 20 cents from $5.10 to $4.90 per bushel. During the same time the price of the December corn futures contract has fallen from $5.50 to $5.32, a decline of 18 cents. The farmer will now sell 75,000 bushels of corn in the spot market at $4.90 and will offset the hedge by purchasing 15 December corn contracts at $5.32. In this case the farmer hedged all but 2 cents of the 20-cent price decline in corn. As a result of the hedge the farmer's effective selling price for the 75,000 bushels of corn is $5.08 per bushel. The effective selling price of $5.08 is found as follows: price of spot corn in October plus profit per bushel on the futures contract ($4.90 + 18 cents = $5.08).

 TAKE**NOTE!**

The effective selling price for a short hedger or producer of the commodity is found using the following formula:

Sale price realized in the spot market +/− profit or loss on the short futures contracts

The effective cost for a long hedger or a user of the commodity is found using the following formula:

The price paid in the spot market +/− the profit or loss on the long futures contracts

HOW TO MANAGE AN IMPERFECT HEDGE

There are a number of factors that can cause a hedge to be less than perfect. In fact, in most cases the hedge is imperfect. Some of the factors that can impact the effectiveness of a hedge are:

- The number of units covered by the futures contract are more or less than the units to be hedged.
- The futures delivery months do not line up with the producer's harvest or production cycle.

- The futures delivery months do not line up with the user's demand cycle.
- The change in the price of the underlying commodity and the change in the price of the futures contract are not perfectly correlated.

While the prices of the commodity and the futures contract converge as the delivery period approaches, a price change in the commodity will not always be completely reflected in the price change of the futures contract and vice versa. As a result, a hedge traditionally will not offset 100% of the losses or 100% of a price increase.

When hedging it is important to select the delivery month that always equals or exceeds the month during which the commodity will be produced or needed. We saw in our second example with the corn farmer that no corn futures contract was trading in April for October delivery. The farmer had to use either the September or December contract. The farmer properly selected the December contract, which exceeded his delivery in October. Had the farmer selected the September contract, the delivery period would have passed and the contract would have expired and left the farmer completely unhedged for weeks into his October harvest and sale. Another challenge can occur when the units to be hedged do not meet the number of units in an even number of contracts. There are no half lots or half contracts in futures. If our corn farmer was predicting that his crop would yield 77,000 bushels of corn it could not be perfectly hedged using corn contracts covering 5,000 bushels of corn. 77,000 bushels ÷ 5,000 bushels per contract would require 15.4 corn contracts to hedge the entire crop. Since the farmer cannot sell 15.4 contracts, he must select either 15 contracts or 16 contracts to hedge his crop. The correct choice for the exam in this type of scenario would be to sell 15 contracts. The Series 3 exam does not want a hedger to over hedge the position. If the farmer sold 16 contracts covering 80,000 bushels, the farmer would have hedged his production and would be speculating on an additional 3,000 bushels.

A CHANGE IN BASIS PRICE

The basis grade is the standard or minimum quality that may be delivered to settle a futures contract. The term *basis* is also used to describe the spread (difference) between the price of the underlying cash commodity and the price of the near-term futures contract. The near term futures contract is the contract with the earliest delivery date and is often referred to as the *front month*. The front month is the contract that is most often quoted and sees most of the trading volume. As the spread or basis changes, the difference between the price of the cash commodity and the price of the front month futures contract narrows or widens. The basis is always quoted as a relationship between the price of the cash commodity and the price of the futures contract. If gold in the spot market is priced at 1,425 and the front month for gold is quoted at 1,440, the basis would be $15 under. If cash gold was at 1,450 and the front month was quoted at 1,440, the basis would be $10 over. The basis and the difference in cash and futures prices can strengthen or weaken depending on the direction of the change in the spread. If the basis (spread between the cash and futures prices) becomes more positive or less negative, the basis is said to strengthen.

EXAMPLE

When the price of gold in the spot market is 1,425 and the price of the futures contract is 1,440, gold is $15 under. If the price of gold moved up to 1,432 and the price of the futures contract moved up to 1,445, gold is now $13 under. The basis has narrowed and has strengthened. The price spread between the cash and futures market (the basis) has become less negative and has moved closer to zero when the basis moved from $15 under to $13 under. If a hedger were to establish a position in both the cash and futures given the above price action, it would look as follows:

Time	Gold Cash/Spot Price	Futures Price	Basis
Hedge established	1,425	1,440	(15)
Hedge reviewed	1,432	1,445	(13)
Change	+7	+5	+2

When the cash price is trading over the futures price, the basis would become stronger if the increase in the price of the cash commodity exceeds the increase in the price of the futures contract. Let's look at a change in the basis when spot gold was trading at 1,450 and the futures were 1,440, $10 over the futures price. If the price of gold moved up to 1,465 and the price of the futures contract moved up to 1,450, gold is now $15 over. The basis has strengthened. The price spread between the cash and futures market (the basis) has become more positive and moved further away from zero when the basis moved from $10 over to $15 over. If a hedger were to establish a position in both the cash and futures given the above price action it would look as follows:

Time	Gold Cash/Spot Price	Futures Price	Basis
Hedge established	1,450	1,440	+10
Hedge reviewed	1,465	1,450	+15
Change	+15	+10	+5

Alternatively, the basis can also weaken when the spread between the price of the cash commodity and the front month futures contract widens or becomes more negative.

If cash corn is trading at 5.10 per bushel and the near-term futures contract is trading at 5.15 per bushel, corn is trading at 5 cents under. If cash corn falls to 4.95 per bushel and the front month falls to 5.09 per bushel, the basis has widened from 5 cents under to 14 cents under. The basis has become more negative and further away from zero. If a hedger were to establish a position in both the cash and futures given the above price action it would look as follows:

Time	Corn Cash/Spot Price	Futures Price	Basis
Hedge established	5.10	5.15	(5)
Hedge reviewed	4.95	5.09	(14)
Change	(15)	(6)	(9)

When the cash price is trading over the futures price the basis would become weaker if the price of the cash commodity falls more than the price of the futures contract. Let's look at a change in the basis when cash corn is trading at 5.25 and the futures are at 5.15, 10 cents over the futures price. If the price of corn fell from 5.25 to 5.18 and the price of the futures contract fell from 5.15 to 5.10, corn is now 8 cents over. The basis has weakened. The price spread between the cash and futures market (the basis) has become less positive and has moved closer to zero when the basis moved from 10 cents over to 8 cents over. If a hedger were to establish a position in both the cash and futures given the above price action, it would look as follows:

Time	Corn Cash/Spot Price	Futures Price	Basis
Hedge established	5.25	5.15	+10
Hedge reviewed	5.18	5.10	+8
Change	−7	−5	(2)

TAKE**NOTE!**

When the price of the cash commodity is trading under the price of the futures contract the commodity is said to have a negative basis. The more negative the spread (further from zero), the weaker the basis becomes. Conversely when the price of the cash commodity is trading over the price of the futures contract the commodity is said to have a positive basis. The more positive the spread (further from zero), the stronger it becomes.

Whether a hedger wants the basis to narrow or to widen, strengthen or weaken depends on the type of hedger they are. Remember there are long hedgers and short hedgers. The following table will detail a basis change for both the long and short hedger.

Hedged Cash Position	Futures Position	Change in Basis	Best Outcome
Long cash commodity Short futures (a producer of the commodity)	Is a short hedger/ sells futures to protect against a price decline	Wants the basis to strengthen, narrow, or become less negative	Wants the price of the commodity to increase and the price of the futures to decline
Short or needs the cash commodity long futures (a user of the commodity)	Is a long hedger/ buys futures to protect against a price increase	Wants the basis to weaken, widen, or become more negative	Wants the price of the commodity to fall and the price of the futures to increase

For a producer of a commodity or for someone who is long the commodity, any profit on the hedge increases the effective selling price for the commodity. Conversely, any loss on the hedge will reduce the effective selling price. For users of the commodity, any gain on the hedge reduces the effective cost for the commodity. Conversely, any loss on the hedge increases the effective cost. Knowing how and when to establish and take off a hedge is extremely important. The ultimate time and price at which the hedge is established or removed dramatically impact its effectiveness.

 TAKE**NOTE!**

While the term basis when quoted in the marketplace refers to the spread between the cash market and the near-term contract, a hedger may establish their own basis by using distant month contracts to establish a hedge.

HEDGING FINANCIAL RISKS

Futures contracts can also be used to hedge a variety of financial risks. Futures contracts are used to hedge everything from a decline in the stock market in the case of a portfolio manager, to currency risk for an import/export business and to interest rate risk for a corporation seeking to raise money through the sale of bonds.

USING INDEX FUTURES AS A HEDGE

In addition to allowing investors to gain exposure to the overall market, the S&P 500 contract allows portfolio managers to efficiently hedge a large diverse portfolio by using S&P futures rather than seeking protection through options for each stock in the portfolio. In the case of a large diverse portfolio, S&P 500 futures contracts are the most efficient hedge against systematic risk. Systematic risk is the risk that is inherent in any investment in the markets. For example, an investor could own stock in the greatest company in the world and could still lose money because the value of the stock is going down, simply because the market as a whole is going down. Portfolio and pension plan managers who manage large portfolios containing many different long stock positions can hedge against the risk of a market decline by selling S&P futures. As the value of the portfolio declines, the profit on the short S&P futures position should offset a significant portion of the loss in market value as a result of systematic risk. Engaging in this type of hedging is sometimes referred to as "portfolio insurance." Nonsystematic risk is the risk that pertains to one company or industry. For example, the problems that the tobacco industry faced a few years ago would not have affected a computer company. Using index futures would not be an effective hedge against nonsystematic risk. Diversification among industries and issuers is the only way to hedge against nonsystematic risk. If a hedge fund is short a significant number of equities, it may seek to hedge against a market rally by purchasing S&P 500 futures. As the value of the short portfolio increases, the profit on the long S&P futures position should offset a significant portion of the loss on the short positions.

EXAMPLE

A pension manager manages the retirement plan for a significant number of workers at a manufacturing company. The total value at risk for the pension plan is approximately $160,000,000. The plan is mostly invested in large cap stocks and the manager is getting concerned that the stock market is due for a pullback and wants to hedge against a decline. Since the plan is mostly invested in large cap stocks, selling S&P 500 futures would be the most effective hedge. The manager now needs to decide how many contracts to sell. With the S&P 500 at 1,600, the total contract value for the futures contract is $400,000, found as follows: $1,600 \times 250 = \$400,000$ contract value. Now the manager must divide the value of the portfolio to be hedged by the value of the S&P contract. In this case

$$\$160,000,000 \div \$400,000 = 400 \text{ contracts}$$

To effectively hedge the $160,000,000 portfolio, the manager must sell 400 S&P futures contracts.

BETA HEDGE

Aggressive managers may have to adjust the value at risk for their portfolios to hedge effectively based on the volatility or beta of their portfolios. A stock's or portfolio's *beta* is its projected rate of change relative to the market as a whole. If the market was up 10% for the year, a stock or portfolio with a beta of 1.5 could reasonably be expected to be up 15%. A stock or portfolio with a beta greater than one has a higher level of volatility than the market as a whole and is considered to be more risky than the overall market. A stock or portfolio with a beta of less than one is less volatile than prices in the overall market and is considered to be less risky. If the $160,000,000 portfolio above had a beta of 1.5, the manager would have to determine the beta-adjusted value at risk by multiplying the $160,000,000 value of the portfolio by the portfolio's beta of 1.5. The beta-adjusted value at risk would now be $240,000,000. Now the manager must divide the beta-adjusted value of the portfolio to be hedged by the value of the S&P contract. In this case

$$\$240,000,000 \div \$400,000 = 600 \text{ contracts}$$

Portfolio managers who oversee portfolios whose holdings may be included in other indexes may choose to hedge using futures on other indexes such as:

- Nasdaq 100
- Dow Jones Industrial Average
- NYSE Composite
- Russell 2,000
- Value Line
- Nikkei 225

An investor who uses index futures to hedge is hedging the systematic risk contained in a portfolio of common stock. An investor who wished to hedge the interest rate risk contained in a portfolio of preferred stock must hedge the risk by taking a position in futures contracts on long term debt securities, such as Treasury bond futures. As interest rates rise the value of the preferred stock will fall as the value of the stated dividend paid on the preferred shares declines as a result of the higher interest rates. To hedge a long portfolio of preferred stock the investor would sell long term debt futures. To hedge a short portfolio of preferred shares an investor would go take a long position in long term debt futures.

ALPHA

A stock's or portfolio's alpha is its projected independent rate of return or the difference between an investment's expected (benchmark) return and its actual return. Portfolio managers whose portfolios have positive alphas are adding value through their asset selection. The outperformance as measured by alpha indicates the portfolio manager is adding additional return for each unit of risk taken on in the portfolio.

CURRENCY HEDGE

Businesses that purchase and sell goods and services internationally may see their earnings impacted by changes in currency valuation. As the value of one currency changes relative to another, profits may decline or costs may increase depending on the type of business and the change in valuation. A strong dollar is good for importers or for businesses that purchase goods from overseas and who purchase these goods in the foreign currency. The risk for a business that needs to make a payment in foreign currency is that the value of the dollar may fall. If the value of the dollar falls it will now take more dollars to purchase the foreign currency, thus making the product more expensive.

A company in this situation would purchase futures on the foreign currency to protect from the value of the dollar falling and would be a long hedger.

EXAMPLE

In September, a business placed an order for a piece of equipment from a German manufacturer. The equipment will be ready for delivery 6 months from now and the order is to be paid for in full in Euros prior to delivery. The price of the equipment is 12,500,000 Euros. To hedge the risk of the Euro rising and to arrange for delivery of the required Euros, the business purchases March Euro futures contracts at 130 when the Euro is trading in the spot market at 128. The contract price represents $1.30 per Euro. Each Euro contract covers 125,000 Euros. The business will have to purchase 100 contracts to hedge the currency risk as follows:

12,500,000 Euros ، 125,000 Euros per contract = 100 contracts

To calculate the total value of the futures contracts, multiply the quoted price by the number of Euros covered in the contract. In this case 1.3 × 125,000 = $162,000 × 100 contracts = $16,200,000.

If the contract delivery period did not match the time when the payment in Euros is due, the company would have to purchase Euros in the spot market and offset the hedge by selling the futures contract. Let's look at the result of the hedge if Euros in the spot market increased from 128 to 131 and the futures contract increased from 1.30 to 132.5. The company must now purchase Euros and offset the hedge.

Time	Euro Spot Price	Futures Price
Hedge established	128	130
Hedge offset	131	132.5
Change	+3 increased cost	+2.5 profit on futures contracts

When the company purchases the Euros in the spot market the total cost has increased to $16,375,000. If the company had not hedged, the cost of the equipment would have increased by $137,500 as a result of the stronger Euro. The hedge was profitable and offset 2.5 cents of the 3-cent increase in the value of the Euro, so the company's effective cost to purchase the Euros was $1.285 or $16,062,500 to purchase 12,500,000 Euros. This is final cost of the equipment.

An exporter who is selling products overseas and who is to receive payments from customers in the foreign currency is concerned that the value of the dollar may rise relative to the value of the foreign currency. If the value of the currency to be received falls, it will purchase fewer U.S. dollars and will reduce the effective sale price of the goods when the foreign currency is converted into dollars. To hedge against this risk, the exporter will sell futures on the foreign currency and is a short hedger.

EXAMPLE

A U.S. exporter is selling goods to a Canadian manufacturer. The payment will be made 6 months from now in 10,000,000 Canadian dollars. To hedge themselves, the U.S. exporter would sell futures on the Canadian dollar to guard against the value of the Canadian dollar declining relative to the U.S. dollar. There are 100,000 Canadian dollars in a Canadian dollar futures contract. The business will have to sell 100 contracts to hedge the currency risk as follows:

10,000,000 Canadian dollars ⸝ 100,000 Canadian dollars per contract

= 100 contracts

At the time the sales contract is signed, the Canadian dollar is trading in the spot market at 98 cents. The U.S. company is concerned that the Canadian dollar may fall between the time the contract is signed and the time when the delivery and payment are made. The company elects to sell 100 June Canadian dollar contracts at 0.99125. When the payment is made in 10,000,000 Canadian dollars, the value of the Canadian dollar has fallen to 97 cents and the June futures contract has fallen to .98250. The company now must convert the Canadian dollars into U.S. dollars and offset the short futures position as follows:

Time	Canadian Dollar Spot Price	Futures Price
Hedge established	.98	.99125
Hedge offset	.97	.98250
Change	−0.01 loss in value	.00875 profit on short futures

The company converts the Canadian dollars to U.S. dollars and receives a total of $9,700,000. The company offsets the hedge by repurchasing the 100 futures contracts, realizing a profit of .00875 or $87,500 for the 100 contracts. Adding this to the total received upon conversion of the Canadian dollars, the total effective selling price in U.S. dollars is $9,785,000. Had the company not hedged the payment in Canadian dollars, the effective sales price would have fallen by $100,000. By hedging with the short futures contract the company offset all but .00125 of the decline.

INTEREST RATE HEDGE

The last hedge we will review is an interest rate hedge. An investor who will have a sum of money to invest at some point in the future and is seeking to invest the money in bonds would be concerned that interest rates may drop by the time the funds are available. If interest rates fall, the price of outstanding bonds will increase. As a result the investor would have to pay more for the bonds and would have a lower current yield and a lower yield to maturity. To hedge against falling interest rates the investor would purchase Treasury bond futures and would be a long hedger.

EXAMPLE

In December, a portfolio manager who has $10,000,000 worth of Treasury bonds maturing in 6 months knows that he will want to reinvest the $10,000,000 principal payment in other Treasury bonds to keep the same asset allocation. The manager is concerned that interest rates may fall from the current attractive level in the market before the bonds mature. To hedge a $10,000,000 investment to be made 6 months in the future and to lock in a desirable rate the manager would purchase 100 June Treasury bond futures contracts. The number of contracts to be purchased is found as follows:

$10,000,000 principal amount to be invested ⏋ $100,000 Treasury futures contract par value = 100 contracts

At the time the manager is looking to hedge, 30-year Treasury bonds are trading in the market at 99.04 and the June futures contract on the Treasury bond is trading at 100.16 with interest rates at approximately 6%. As the time approaches for the manager to receive the principal payment on the maturing bonds, investors have bid up the price of bonds and interest rates have fallen. If the manager's principal payment is received during the delivery period of the futures contract the manager may simply elect to accept delivery of the bonds. However, if the principal payment and the delivery period do not occur at the same time, the manager will have to purchase bonds in the spot market and offset the hedge. As interest rates have fallen from slightly over 6% to approximately 5.93%, the price of Treasury bonds in the spot market has increased from 99.04 to 101.04. At the same time the price of the Treasury bond futures contract has increased from 100.16 to 102.16. The portfolio manager will now have to buy the bonds in the spot market and offset the hedge by selling the futures contracts as follows:

Time	Treasury Bonds Spot Price	Futures Price
Hedge established	99.04	100.16
Hedge offset	101.04	102.16
Change	+2 increase in bond price	+2 profit on futures contract

When the manager receives the $10,000,000 principal payment he will purchase Treasury bonds in the spot market at 101-4/32 % × $10,000,000 = 101.125 % × $10,000,000 = $10,112,500. The price of the bonds increased by $200,000 from $9,912,500 to $10,112,500 as interest rates fell. The manager will now sell the 100 Treasury bond futures contract at a $200,000 profit and has completely hedged the increased price.

A company that knows it will need to borrow money in the future through the issuance (sale) of bonds would be concerned that interest rates would increase and that the company would have to pay a higher rate of interest on its debt securities. To hedge the risk of rising interest rates the company would sell Treasury bond futures and would be a short hedger.

EXAMPLE ABC Mills, a timber company, wants to renovate one of their mills after the next logging season 12 months from now. ABC needs $10,000,000 to renovate the mill and is planning on offering bonds to finance the work. The registration statement for the bond offering is just getting started and will take some time to complete. ABC is concerned that interest rates may rise and the selling price of the bonds will be lower than they would be if ABC were able to sell the bonds today. ABC is now looking to hedge its future borrowing cost and wants to establish an anticipatory hedge using T bond futures. At the time the hedge is established corporate bonds are selling in the market at a price equivalent to 98.16. To hedge a $10,000,000 bond offering to be made 12 months in the future and to lock in a desirable rate the company would sell 100 Treasury bond futures contracts. The number of contracts to be sold is found as follows:

$10,000,000 principal amount to be borrowed ⌿ $100,000 Treasury futures contract par value = 100 contracts

At the time ABC is looking to hedge, similar corporate bonds are trading in the market at a price equivalent to 98.16 and the futures contract on the Treasury bond is trading at 107.16. As the time approaches for ABC to issue the bonds, interest rates have risen and the price of bonds has fallen. ABC offers the bonds for sale at a price equal to 94.16 and at the same time will offset the hedge by repurchasing the Treasury contracts. The price of the Treasury futures contract has also fallen from 107.16 to 103.24. ABC offsets the hedge as follows:

Time	Corporate Bonds Spot Price	Treasury Futures Price
Hedge established	98.16	107.16
Hedge offset	94.16	103.24
Change	4 decline in price	+3-24/32 profit on futures contract.

ABC sells the $10,000,000 worth of bonds at 94.16 or 94-16/32% and receives $9,450,000, found as follows:

$$94.16 = 94 \text{-} 16/32\% = 94.5\% \times \$10,000,000 = \$9,450,000$$

If ABC did not hedge the offering, the proceeds from the sale would be $400,000 lower than what could have been received 12 months earlier. However ABC sold 100 Treasury bonds futures contracts and made 3-24/32 or 3.75% × 10,000,000 = $375,000, so the effective sale price that ABC realized on the sale of its bonds is 94.16 + 3.24 = 97-40/32 = 98.08 for total proceeds of $9,825,000, found as follows:

$$98.08 = 98 \text{-} 8/32\% = 98.25\%$$

$$98.25\% \; ' \; \$10,000,000 = \$9,825,000$$

TAKENOTE!

Anticipatory hedges are established to reduce the risks of unknown future events not to hedge the price risk associated with a current position in a commodity or security.

An anticipatory hedge would be established by all of the following:

A person who needs to buy a commodity in the future

A person who wants to purchase bonds or stock in the future

A corporation looking to borrow money through the sale of bonds in the future

Pretest

1. The motive of a hedger is to realize a profit on a position in a futures contract based on change in the value of the futures contract.

    True

    False

2. An oil trader executes the following orders for crude (1,000 barrels per contract) 3 weeks apart:

    Bought 3 December crude oil at 92.50

    Sold 3 December crude oil at 94.25

    His profit or loss on the trade is:

    a. $1,750 profit.

    b. $3,500 profit.

    c. $5,250 profit.

    d. $6,250 profit.

3. To determine the profit or loss on a trade in a gold futures contract, the profit or loss must be multiplied by:

    a. 1,000 ounces.

    b. 1,000 troy ounces.

    c. 100 ounces.

    d. 100 troy ounces.

4. Initial margin to carry a futures position is:

    a. Set by the CFTC and is the same for both long and short contracts.

    b. Set by the CFTC and varies for long and short contracts.

    c. Set by the exchange and is the same for both long and short contracts.

    d. Set by the exchange and varies for long and short contracts.

5. A trader who feels that the price of gold will fall sells 1 October gold (100 Troy ounces) at 1425 and deposits the required margin of $75 per ounce. Gold increases in price to 1431. The trader's margin equity in the account at this level is:

    a. $6,900.

    b. $69,000.

    c. $8,100.

    d. $81,000.

6. The open trade equity in a trader's account is calculated based on

    a. The maintenance margin plus or minus the realized profit and loss.

    b. The maintenance margin plus or minus the unrealized profit and loss.

    c. The initial margin plus or minus the realized profit and loss.

    d. The initial margin plus or minus the unrealized profit and loss.

7. Hedgers take futures positions that are in the same direction as their position in the underlying cash commodity.

    True

    False

8. In March the price of wheat in the cash market is 5.08 per bushel. A storage operator with 100,000 bushels of wheat on hand is concerned about the price of wheat falling and wants to hedge their wheat inventory. The storage operator sells 20 July wheat at 5.19. Just prior to the beginning of the delivery period in July the storage operator sells his 100,000 bushels of wheat in the cash market at 5.11 and offsets his July futures at 5.14. What was the operator's effective selling price per bushel?

    a. 5.17

    b. 5.29

    c. 5.13

    d. 5.16

9. If cash corn is trading at 4.70 per bushel and the near-term futures contract is trading at 4.82 per bushel, corn is trading at 12 cents over.

   True

   False

10. Someone who is short or needs the cash commodity and is long futures would have the best outcome if:

   a. The price of the cash commodity falls and the price of the futures fall.

   b. The price of the cash commodity rises and the price of the futures rise.

   c. The price of the cash commodity falls and the price of the futures rise.

   d. The price of the cash commodity rises and the price of the futures fall.

Commodity Futures Options and Commodity Futures Spreads

INTRODUCTION

A commodity futures option is a contract between two parties that determines the time and price at which a futures contract may be bought or sold. The two parties to the contract are the buyer and the seller. The buyer of the option pays money, known as the option's premium, to the seller. For this premium, the buyer obtains a right to buy or sell the contract depending on what type of option is involved in the transaction. The seller, because they received the premium from the buyer, now has an obligation to perform under that contract. Depending on the option involved, the seller may have an obligation to buy or sell the futures contract.

OPTION CLASSIFICATION

Options are classified as to their type, class, and series. There are two types of options: calls and puts.

CALL OPTIONS

A call option gives the buyer the right to buy or to *call* the futures contract from the option seller at a specific price for a certain period of time. The sale of a call option obligates the seller to deliver or sell that futures contract to the buyer at that specific price for a certain period of time.

PUT OPTIONS

A put option gives the buyer the right to sell or to *put* the futures contract to the seller at a specific price for a certain period of time. The sale of a put option obligates the seller to buy the futures contract from the buyer at that specific price for a certain period of time.

OPTION CLASSES

An option class consists of all options of the same type for the same underlying futures contract.

For example, all crude calls would be one class of options and all crude puts would be another class of option.

Class 1	Class 2
Crude June 50 calls	Crude June 50 puts
Crude June 55 calls	Crude June 55 puts
Crude July 50 calls	Crude July 50 puts
Crude July 55 calls	Crude July 55 puts
Crude August 50 calls	Crude August 50 puts

OPTION SERIES

An option series is the most specific classification of options and consists of only options of the same class with the same exercise price and expiration month. For example, all Crude June 50 calls would be one series of options and all Crude June 55 calls would be another series of options.

BULLISH VS. BEARISH

BULLISH

Investors who believe that a futures contract's price will increase over time are said to be bullish. Investors who buy calls are bullish on the underlying futures contract. That is, they believe that the futures contract price will rise and have paid for the right to purchase the futures contract at a specific price known as the exercise price or strike price. An investor who has sold puts is also considered to be bullish on the futures contract. The seller of a put has an obligation to buy the futures contract and, therefore, believes that the futures contract price will rise.

BEARISH

Investors who believe that a futures contract's price will decline are said to be bearish. The seller of a call has an obligation to sell the futures contract to the purchaser at a specified price and believes that the futures contract's price will fall and is therefore bearish. The buyer of a put wants the price to drop so that they may sell the futures contract at a higher price to the seller of the put contract. They are also considered to be bearish on the futures contract.

	Calls	**Puts**
Buyers	Bullish	Bearish
	Have right to buy futures contract, want futures contract price to rise	Have right to sell futures contract, want futures contract price to fall
Sellers	Bearish	Bullish
	Have obligation to sell futures contract, want futures contract price to fall	Have obligation to buy futures contract, want futures contract price to rise

Buyer vs. Seller

Buyer		**Seller**
Owner	Known as	Writer
Long	Known as	Short
Rights	Has	Obligations
Maximum Speculative Profit	Objective	Premium Income
With an opening purchase	Enters the contract	With an opening sale
	Wants the option to	
Exercise		Expire

POSSIBLE OUTCOMES FOR AN OPTION

EXERCISED

If the option is exercised, the buyer has elected to exercise their rights to buy or sell the futures contract, depending on the type of option involved. Exercising an option obligates the seller to perform under the contract. Option contracts may be established as either American or European exercise. American style options may be exercised anytime during the life of the option. A European style option may only be exercised at expiration.

SOLD

Most individual investors will elect to sell their rights to another investor rather than exercise their rights. The investor who buys the option from them will acquire all the rights of the original purchaser.

EXPIRE

If the option expires, the buyer has elected not to exercise their right and the seller of the option is relieved of their obligation to perform.

EXERCISE PRICE

The exercise price is the price at which an option buyer may buy or sell the underlying futures contract, depending on the type of option involved in the transaction. The exercise price is also known as the strike price.

MANAGING AN OPTION POSITION

Both the buyer and seller, in an option trade, establish the position with an opening transaction. The buyer has an opening purchase and the seller has an opening sale. To exit the option position, an investor must *close out* the position. The buyer of the option may exit their position through:

- A closing sale.
- Exercising the option.
- Allowing the option to expire.

The seller of an option may exit or close out their position through:

- A closing purchase.
- Having the option exercised or assigned to them.
- Allowing the option to expire.

Most individual investors do not exercise their options and will simply buy and sell options in much the same way as they would buy or sell futures contracts.

BUYING CALLS

An investor who purchases a call believes that the underlying contract price will rise and that they will be able to profit from the price appreciation by purchasing calls. Call options on futures contracts can also be used by hedgers who need to purchase the commodity in the future as a way to protect against a rise in the price of the needed commodity. An investor who purchases a call can control the underlying futures contract and profit from its appreciation while limiting their loss to the amount of the premium paid for the calls. Buying calls allows the investor to maximize their leverage and they may realize a more significant percentage return based on their investment. An investor may also elect to purchase a call to lock in a purchase price for a futures contract if the investor currently lacks the funds required to purchase the contract, but will have the funds available in the near future. When looking to establish a position the buyer must determine:

- Their maximum gain.
- Their maximum loss.
- Their breakeven.

MAXIMUM GAIN LONG CALLS

When an investor has a long call position, their maximum gain is always unlimited. They profit from a rise in the price of the futures contract. Since there is no limit to how high the price of a futures contract may rise, their maximum gain is unlimited just as if they had purchased the futures contract.

MAXIMUM LOSS LONG CALLS

Whenever an investor is long, or owns a futures contract, their maximum loss can be significant if the price of the contract falls dramatically. When an investor purchases a call option, the amount they pay for the option or their premium is always going to be their maximum loss.

DETERMINING THE BREAKEVEN FOR LONG CALLS

An investor who has purchased calls must determine where the futures contract price must be at expiration in order for the investor to break even on the transaction. An investor who has purchased calls has paid the premium to the seller in the hopes that the price of the futures contract will rise. The futures contract must appreciate by enough to cover the cost of the investor's option premium in order for them to break even at expiration. To determine an investor's breakeven point on a long call, use the following formula:

breakeven = strike price + premium

EXAMPLE

An investor has established the following option position:

Long 1 December gold 1300 call at 3

The investor's maximum gain, maximum loss, and breakeven will be:

Maximum gain: Unlimited

Maximum loss: $300 (The amount of the premium paid × 100 troy ounces)

Breakeven : $1303 = 1030 + 3 (Strike price + premium)

If at expiration December gold is at exactly $1303 and the investor sells or exercises their option, they will break even, excluding transactions costs.

SELLING CALLS

An investor who sells a call believes that the underlying contract price will fall and that they will be able to profit from a decline in the futures price by selling calls. An investor who sells a call is obligated to deliver the underlying contract if the buyer decides to exercise the option. When looking to establish a position, the seller must determine:

- Their maximum gain.
- Their maximum loss.
- Their breakeven.

MAXIMUM GAIN SHORT CALLS

For an investor who has sold uncovered or naked calls, maximum gain is always limited to the amount of the premium they received when they sold the calls.

MAXIMUM LOSS SHORT CALLS

An investor who has sold uncovered or naked calls does not own the underlying futures contract and, as a result, has unlimited risk and the potential for an unlimited loss. The seller of the calls is subject to a loss if the price of the futures contract increases. Since there is no limit to how high a futures contract price may rise, there is no limit to the amount of their loss.

DETERMINING THE BREAKEVEN FOR SHORT CALLS

An investor who has sold calls must determine where the futures contract price must be at expiration in order for the investor to break even on the transaction. An investor who has sold calls has received the premium from the buyer in the hopes that the futures contract price will fall. If the futures contract appreciates, the investor may begin to lose money. The futures contract price may appreciate by the amount of the option premium received and the investor will still break even at expiration. To determine an investor's breakeven point on a short call, use the following formula:

breakeven = strike price + premium

EXAMPLE

An investor has established the following option position:

Short 1 December gold 1300 call at 3

The investor's maximum gain, maximum loss, and breakeven will be:

Maximum gain: $300 (The amount of the premium received)
Maximum loss: Unlimited
Breakeven: $1303 = 1300 + 3 (Strike price + premium)

If at expiration December gold is at exactly $1303 and the investor closes out the transaction with a closing purchase or has the option exercised against them, they will break even, excluding transactions costs.

Notice the relationship between the buyer and the seller:

	Call Buyer	Call Seller
Maximum gain	Unlimited	Premium received
Maximum loss	Premium paid	Unlimited
Breakeven	Strike price + premium	Strike price + premium
Wants option to	Exercise	Expire

Because an option is a two-party contract, the buyer's maximum gain is the seller's maximum loss and the buyer's maximum loss is the seller's maximum gain. Both the buyer and the seller will break even at the same point.

BUYING PUTS

An investor who purchases a put believes that the underlying futures contract price will fall and that they will be able to profit from a decline in the price of the futures contract by purchasing puts. Put options on futures contracts can also be used by hedgers who need to sell the commodity in the future as a way to protect against a fall in the price of the commodity. An investor who purchases a put can control the underlying futures contract and profit from its price decline while limiting their loss to the amount of the premium paid for the puts. Buying puts allows the investor to maximize their leverage while limiting their losses and the investor may realize a more significant percentage return based on their investment when compared to the return that could be realized from shorting a futures contract. When looking to establish a position the buyer must determine:

- Their maximum gain.
- Their maximum loss.
- Their breakeven.

MAXIMUM GAIN LONG PUTS

An investor who has purchased a put believes that the futures contract price will fall. There is, however, a limit to how far a futures contract price may decline. A futures contract price may never fall below zero. As a result, the investor who believes that the futures contract price will fall has a limited maximum gain. To determine the maximum gain for the buyer of a put, use the following formula:

maximum gain = strike price − premium

MAXIMUM LOSS LONG PUTS

Whenever an investor is short a futures contract, their maximum loss is always unlimited because there is no limit to how high the price of a futures contract may go. When an investor purchases a put option, the amount they pay for the option or their premium is always going to be their maximum loss.

DETERMINING THE BREAKEVEN
FOR LONG PUTS

Whenever an investor has purchased a put, they believe that the futures contract price will decline. In order for the investor to break even on the transaction, the futures contract price must fall by enough to offset the amount of the premium paid for the option. At expiration the investor will break even at the following point:

breakeven = strike price − premium

Example   An investor has established the following option position:

Long 1 June crude oil 70 put at .5

The investor's maximum gain, maximum loss, and breakeven will be:

Maximum gain: $69.5 or $69,500 for the whole position (strike price − premium)

Maximum loss: $500 (The amount of the premium paid, 50 cents × 1000 barrels)

Breakeven = $69.5 = 70 − .50 (strike price − premium)

If at expiration June crude oil is at exactly $69.50 and the investor sells or exercises their option, they will break even, excluding transactions costs.

SELLING PUTS

An investor who sells a put believes that the underlying futures contract price will rise and that they will be able to profit from a rise in the futures contract price by selling puts. An investor who sells a put is obligated to purchase the underlying futures contract if the buyer decides to exercise the option. An investor who sells a put may also be selling the put as a way to acquire the underlying contract at a cheaper price. If the futures contract is put to the investor, the investor's purchase price is reduced by the amount of the premium received. When looking to establish a position the seller must determine:

- Their maximum gain.
- Their maximum loss.
- Their breakeven.

MAXIMUM GAIN SHORT PUTS

For an investor who has sold uncovered or naked puts, maximum gain is always limited to the amount of the premium they received when they sold the puts.

MAXIMUM LOSS SHORT PUTS

An investor who has sold a put believes that the futures contract price will rise. There is, however, a limit to how far a futures contract price may decline. A futures contract price may never fall below zero. As a result, the investor who believes that the futures contract price will rise and has sold puts has a limited maximum loss. The worst thing that can happen for an investor who is short a put is that the futures contract goes to zero and they are forced to purchase it at the strike price from the owner of the put. To determine the maximum loss for the seller of a put, use the following formula:

maximum loss = strike price − premium

DETERMINING THE BREAKEVEN FOR SHORT PUTS

Whenever an investor has sold a put, they believe that the futures contract price will rise. If the futures contract price begins to fall, the investor becomes subject to a loss. In order for the investor to break even on the transaction, the futures contract price must fall by the amount of the premium they received for the option. At expiration the investor will break even at the following point:

breakeven = strike price – premium

EXAMPLE

An investor has established the following option position:

Short 1 June crude 70 put at .50

The investor's maximum gain, maximum loss, and breakeven will be:

Maximum gain: $500 (The amount of the premium received 50 cents × 1,000 barrels of crude)

Maximum loss: $69.50 or $69,500 for the whole position (strike price – premium)

Breakeven = $69.50 = 70 – .50 (strike price – premium)

If at expiration June crude is at exactly $69.5 and the investor closes out the position with a closing purchase or has the option exercised against them, they will break even, excluding transactions costs.

Notice the relationship between the buyer and the seller:

	Put Buyer	Put Seller
Maximum gain	Strike price – premium	Premium received
Maximum loss	Premium paid	Strike price – premium
Breakeven	Strike price – premium	Strike price – premium
Wants option to	Exercise	Expire

Because an option is a two-party contract, the buyer's maximum gain is the seller's maximum loss and the buyer's maximum loss is the seller's maximum gain. Both the buyer and the seller will break even at the same point.

OPTION PREMIUMS

The price of an option is known as its premium. Factors that determine the value of an option and, as a result, its premium are:

- The relationship of the underlying futures contract price to the option's strike price.
- The amount of time to expiration.
- The volatility of the underlying futures contract.
- Supply and demand.
- Interest rates.

An option can be:

- In the money.
- At the money.
- Out of the money.

These terms describe the relationship between the price of the underlying futures contract to the option's strike price. These terms do not describe how profitable the position is.

IN-THE-MONEY OPTIONS

A call is in the money when the price of the underlying futures contract is greater than the call's strike price.

| EXAMPLE | A May 550 corn call is 15 cents in the money when May corn is at $5.65 per bushel.
A put is in the money when the price of the underlying futures contract is lower than the put's strike price. |

| EXAMPLE | A May 550 corn put is 10 cents in the money when May corn is at $5.40 per bushel.
It would only make sense to exercise an option if it was in the money. |

AT-THE-MONEY OPTIONS

Both puts and calls are at the money when the price of the underlying futures contract equals the option's exercise price.

| EXAMPLE | If December crude is trading at $60 per barrel, all of the December crude 60 calls and all of the December crude 60 puts will be at the money. |

OUT-OF-THE-MONEY OPTIONS

A call is out of the money when the price of the underlying futures contract is lower than the option's strike price.

EXAMPLE An October gold 1250 call is out of the money when October gold is trading at $1220 per ounce.

A put option is out of the money when the price of the underlying futures contract is above the option's strike price.

EXAMPLE An October gold 1200 put is out of the money when October gold is trading at $1220 per ounce.

It would not make sense to exercise an out-of-the-money option.

	Calls	Puts
In the money	Futures contract price > strike price	Futures contract price < strike price
At the money	Futures contract price = strike price	Futures contract price = strike price
Out of the money	Futures contract price < strike price	Futures contract price > strike price

INTRINSIC VALUE AND TIME VALUE

An option's total premium is comprised of intrinsic value and time value. An option's intrinsic value is equal to the amount the option is in the money. Time value is the amount by which an option's premium exceeds its intrinsic value. In effect, the time value is the price an investor pays for the opportunity to exercise the option. An option that is out of the money has no intrinsic value; therefore, the entire premium consists of time value.

EXAMPLE A June crude 70 call is trading at $2 when June crude is trading at $68 per barrel. The June 70 call is out of the money and has no intrinsic value; therefore, the entire $2 premium consists of time value. If a June crude 65 put is trading at $3 when June crude is at $66 per barrel, the entire $3 is time value.

If in the above example the options were in the money and the premium exceeded the intrinsic value of the option, the remaining premium would be time value.

EXAMPLE A June crude 70 call is trading at $2 when June crude is trading at $70.50 The June 70 call is in the money and has 50 cents in intrinsic value; therefore, the rest of the premium consists of the time value of $1.50. If June crude 65 put is trading at $3 when June crude is trading at $63, the put is in the money by $2 and the rest of the premium or $1 is time value.

PREMIUMS FOR OPTIONS ON TREASURY BOND FUTURES

Treasury bond futures are priced as a percentage of par down to 32nds of 1%. Options on Treasury futures are also quoted as a percentage of par down, but are priced in increments of 64ths of 1%.

| **EXAMPLE** | A May Treasury bond futures 103 call is quoted at 1.32. The premium is calculated as follows: |

$$1.32 = 1\text{-}32/64\% \times \$100,000$$

$$1.5\% \text{ ´ } \$100,000 = \$1,500$$

The investor will pay $1,500 for the right to purchase the May Treasury bond future at 103.

PREMIUMS FOR OPTIONS ON TREASURY BILL FUTURES

Options for Treasury bill futures are based on $1,000,000 par value of a 13-week Treasury bill that has yet to be issued. The option's premium is quoted in points and basis points as an annualized percentage of the $1,000,000 par value. Because there are four 13-week quarters in a year, the premium would have to be divided by four to determine the amount owed or due.

| **EXAMPLE** | A price-based Treasury bill futures option is quoted at 1% |

$$1\% \text{ ´ } \$1,000,000 = \$10,000$$

$$\$10,000 \text{ , } 4 = \$2,500$$

In this case, the investor would pay $2,500 to purchase the Treasury bill futures option.

MULTIPLE OPTION POSITIONS AND STRATEGIES

Option strategies that contain positions in more than one option can be used effectively by investors to meet their objective and to profit from movement in the price of the underlying futures contract.

LONG STRADDLES

A long straddle is the simultaneous purchase of a call and a put on the same futures contract with the same strike price and expiration month. An option investor would purchase a straddle when they expect the futures contract price to be extremely volatile and to make a significant move in either direction. An investor who owns a straddle is neither bullish nor bearish. They are not concerned with whether the futures contract moves up or down in price so long as it moves significantly. An investor may purchase a straddle just prior to a significant announcement such as a crop report or the release of minutes of the Federal Reserve Board with the belief that the announcement will cause the price of the underlying futures contract to appreciate or decline significantly. Before an investor establishes a long straddle, they must determine the following:

- Their maximum gain
- Their maximum loss
- Their breakeven

Let's look at an example.

EXAMPLE   September corn is trading at $5 per bushel and the crop report is due out at the end of the week. An investor feels that if the crop report projects reduced production, the price of corn will increase significantly. However, if the crop report is in line with estimates, corn prices will fall dramatically. An investor with the above opinion establishes the following position:

Long 1 September corn 500 call at .15
Long 1 September corn 500 put at .12

MAXIMUM GAIN LONG STRADDLE

Because the investor in a long straddle owns the calls, the investor's maximum gain is always going to be unlimited.

MAXIMUM LOSS LONG STRADDLE

An investor's maximum loss on a long straddle is limited to the total premium paid for the straddle. The total premium is found using the following formula:

total premium = call premium + put premium

Let's look at the straddle established by our corn trader.

EXAMPLE

Long 1 September corn 500 call at .15

Long 1 September corn 500 put at .12

To determine the investor's maximum loss, simply add the premiums together.

$15 + 12 = 27$

The investor's maximum loss is 27 cents per bushel or $1,350 for the entire position, found as follows:

total premium of 27 cents ´ 5,000 bushels = $1,350

The investor will only realize their maximum loss on a long straddle if the price of the futures contract at expiration is exactly equal to the strike price of both the call and put and both options expire worthless. If, at expiration, September corn closes at exactly $5, or 500 cents, the investor in this case will suffer their maximum possible loss.

DETERMINING THE BREAKEVEN FOR LONG STRADDLE

Because the position contains both a put and a call, the investor is going to have two breakeven points, one breakeven for the call side of the straddle and one for the put side.

To determine the breakeven point for the call side of the straddle, use the following formula:

breakeven = call strike price + total premium

EXAMPLE

Long 1 September corn 500 call at .15

Long 1 September corn 500 put at .12

Total premium = 27

$500 + 27 = 527$

The investor will break even if September corn appreciates to $5.27 per bushel at expiration. The price of the futures contract has to appreciate by enough to offset the total premium cost.

Alternatively, to determine the breakeven point for the put side of the straddle, use the following formula:

breakeven = put strike price – total premium

 **500 ▢ 27 = 473**

If September corn was to fall to $4.73 per bushel at expiration, the investor would break even. The price of the futures contract would have to fall by enough to offset the total premium cost. If the contract price appreciated past $5.27 per bushel or was to fall below $4.73 per bushel, the position would become profitable for the investor.

> ## 🔆 FOCUSPOINT!
>
> An investor who is long a straddle wants the price of the futures contract outside of their breakeven points. In the above case, that would be either above $5.27 per bushel or below $4.73 per bushel.

SHORT STRADDLES

A short straddle is the simultaneous sale of a call and a put on the same futures contract with the same strike price and expiration month. An option investor would sell a straddle when they expect the price of a futures contact to trade within a narrow range or to become less volatile and to not make a significant move in either direction. An investor who is short a straddle is neither bullish nor bearish. They are not concerned with whether the price of the futures contract moves up or down in price, so long as it does not move significantly. An investor may sell a straddle just after a period of high volatility with the belief that the price of the futures contract will now move sideways for a period of time. Before an investor establishes a short straddle, they must determine the following:

- Their maximum gain
- Their maximum loss
- Their breakeven

MAXIMUM GAIN SHORT STRADDLE

An investor's maximum gain with a short straddle is always going to be limited to the amount of the premium received. Let's look at the same position from before, only this time let's look at it from the seller's point of view.

EXAMPLE

> Short 1 September corn 500 call at .15
>
> Short 1 September corn 500 put at .12
>
> To determine the investor's maximum gain, simply add the premiums together
>
> $15 + 12 = 27$
>
> The investor's maximum gain is 27 cents per bushel or $1,350 for the entire position, found as follows:
>
> 27 cents per bushel ´ 5,000 bushels = $1,350

An investor who is short a straddle will only realize their maximum gain if the price of the futures contract closes at the strike price at expiration and both options expire worthless. In this case, if September corn closes at exactly $5 or 500 cents, the investor will have a $1,350 profit on the entire position.

MAXIMUM LOSS SHORT STRADDLE

Because the investor in a short straddle is short the calls, the investor's maximum loss is always going to be unlimited. The loss is unlimited because there is no limit to how high the price of a futures contract can go.

DETERMINING THE BREAKEVEN FOR SHORT STRADDLE

Just like with a long straddle, the investor is going to have two breakeven points, one breakeven for the call side of the straddle and one for the put side.

To determine the breakeven point for the call side of the straddle, use the following formula:

breakeven = call strike price + total premium

Using the same example, we get:

EXAMPLE

> Short 1 September corn 500 call at .15
>
> Short 1 September corn 500 put at .12

Total premium = 27

$$50 + 27 = 527$$

The investor will break even if September corn appreciates to $5.27 per bushel at expiration. Alternatively, to determine the breakeven point for the put side of the straddle, use the following formula:

breakeven = put strike price – total premium

500 □ 27 = 473

If September corn was to fall to $4.73 per bushel at expiration, the investor would break even. If September corn appreciated past $5.27 per bushel or was to fall below $4.73 per bushel, the investor would begin to lose money.

 FOCUSPOINT!

An investor who is short a straddle wants the price of the futures contract inside of their breakeven points. In the above case, that would be either below $5.27 per bushel or above $4.73 per bushel.

Position	Max Gain	Max Loss	Breakeven	At Expiration
Long straddle	Unlimited	Total premium	Strike price + or – total premium	Profitable if outside breakeven
Short straddle	Total premium	Unlimited	Strike price + or – total premium	Profitable if inside breakeven

 TESTTIP!

To help you remember where an investor wants price of the futures contract to be at expiration, use the mnemonic device for straddles SILO: Short Inside Long Outside.

SPREADS

A spread is created through the simultaneous purchase and sale of two options of the same class with different exercise prices, expiration months, or both. There are several different types of spreads that may be created using either calls or puts. They are:

- Price spread/Vertical spread/Money spread
- Calendar spread/Time spread/Horizontal spread
- Diagonal spread

PRICE SPREAD/VERTICAL SPREAD

A price spread or vertical spread consists of 1 long option and 1 short option of the same class with different strike prices. The position is normally called a price spread because of the difference in strike prices between the long and short options. It may also be called a vertical spread because of the way the options are listed in the option chain or in the newspaper. A price spread could be established in either calls or puts as follows:

EXAMPLE

Long 1 March wheat 400 call

Short 1 March wheat 550 call

A price spread could also be established using puts:

Long 1 March wheat 600 put

Short 1 March wheat 550 put

CALENDAR SPREAD/TIME SPREAD

A calendar spread or time spread contains one long option and one short option of the same class with different expiration months. It may also be called a horizontal spread because of how the options are listed in the option chain or in the newspaper.

EXAMPLE

Short 1 April gold 1300 call

Long 1 August gold 1300 call

A time spread could also be established using puts:

Short 1 July soybean 800 put

Long 1 September soybean 800 put

DIAGONAL SPREAD

A diagonal spread consists of 1 long option and 1 short option of the same class that have different strike prices and expiration months. The position is called a diagonal spread because of the way the options are listed in the option chain or in the newspaper.

EXAMPLE

Short 1 May feeder cattle 80 call

Long 1 September feeder cattle 70 call

A diagonal spread could also be established using puts:

Short 1 September S&P 500 1400 put

Long 1 December S&P 500 1450 put

ANALYZING SPREADS/PRICE SPREADS

An investor who is bullish or bearish can use spreads to profit from their opinion about prices in the market place. We will use price spreads to determine:

- If the investor is bullish or bearish.
- If the position has resulted in a net debit or credit.
- The maximum gain.
- The maximum loss.
- The breakeven point.
- If the investor wants the options to be exercised or to expire.
- If the investor wants the difference in the premiums to widen or narrow.

BULL CALL SPREADS/DEBIT CALL SPREADS

To establish a bull call spread, the investor purchases the call with the lower strike price and simultaneously sells the call with the higher strike price. An investor who believes that the price of the futures contract will rise may purchase the call with the lower strike price and sell the call with the higher strike price to offset the risk of losing all of the premium paid for the long call. A bull call spread will always be a debit spread because the right to purchase a futures contract at a lower price for the same amount of time will always be worth more than the right to purchase the same futures contract at a higher price.

A bull call spread could be established as follows:

Long 1 April feeder cattle 80 call at .08

Short 1 April feeder cattle 90 call at .02

By selling the April 90 call, the investor has reduced their maximum loss from 8 cents per pound to 6 cents per pound. Or from $4,000 to $3,000, found as follows:

April 80 call option premium 8 cents × 50,000 lbs = $4,000

April 90 call option premium 2 cents × 50,000 lbs = $1,000

Net premium paid $3,000

By selling the April 90 call, the investor has also limited their upside potential on the position.

Before entering into a bull call spread, the investor must determine:

- Their maximum gain.
- Their maximum loss.
- Their breakeven.

MAXIMUM GAIN BULL CALL SPREAD

The investor's maximum gain on a bull call spread has been limited because they sold the call with the higher strike price. Any appreciation past the strike price of the short call will belong to the investor who purchased the call. To determine the maximum gain on a bull call spread, use the following formula:

difference in the strike price – net premium paid

Using the same example, we get:

Long 1 April feeder cattle 80 call at .08

Short 1 April feeder cattle 90 call at .02

$10 \square 6 = 4$

The investor's maximum gain is 4 cents per pound or $2,000, found as follows: 4 cents × 50,000 lbs = $2,000 for the entire position. The investor will realize their maximum gain if both options are exercised.

MAXIMUM LOSS BULL CALL SPREAD

An investor who is long a bull call spread has a maximum loss equal to the amount of the net premium paid for the spread. An investor will realize their maximum loss if both options expire worthless.

DETERMINING THE BREAKEVEN FOR A BULL CALL SPREAD

To determine where the futures contract has to be at expiration for the investor to break even, use the following formula:

lower strike price + net premium

Using the same example, we get:

Long 1 April feeder cattle 80 call at .08

Short 1 April feeder cattle 90 call at .02

$80 + 6 = 86$

If, at expiration, April feeder cattle is at 86 cents per pound, the investor will break even on the position, excluding transaction costs. If the price of the futures contract is higher than 86 cents, the investor will make money. If it is lower than 86 cents, the investor will lose money.

SPREAD PREMIUMS BULL CALL SPREAD

An investor who has established a bull call spread has bought the spread and paid a net premium to establish the position. The investor will realize a profit on the spread if the difference in the premiums increases or widens. Let's look at our example again:

Long 1 April feeder cattle 80 call at .08

Short 1 April feeder cattle 90 call at .02

The difference between the premium on the long April 80 call and the short April 90 call is 6 cents. If the difference in the value of the premiums increases or widens, the investor will make money. Let's look at the value of the same spread at expiration given different closing prices for April feeder cattle

	Opened at	Cattle at 87	Cattle at 92	Cattle at 79
Long 1 April feeder cattle 80 call	.08	7	12	0
Short 1 April feeder cattle 90 call	.02	0	2	0
Difference	.06	7	10	0
Profit/Loss	N/A	$500	$2,000	($3,000)

Notice that the difference between the premiums can never widen past the amount of the spread. This is a 10-point spread; therefore, the difference between the value of the premiums may never widen past 10.

BEAR CALL SPREADS/CREDIT CALL SPREADS

To establish a bear call spread, the investor sells the call with the lower strike price and simultaneously buys the call with the higher strike price. An investor who believes that the price of the futures contract will fall may sell the call with the lower strike price and purchase the call with the higher strike price to ensure that their maximum loss is not unlimited. A bear call spread or credit call spread could be established as follows:

Short 1 April feeder cattle 80 call at .08

Long 1 April feeder cattle 90 call at .02

Before entering into a bear call spread, the investor must determine:

- Their maximum gain.
- Their maximum loss.
- Their breakeven.

MAXIMUM GAIN BEAR CALL SPREAD/ CREDIT CALL SPREAD

The maximum gain for a bear call spread is equal to the net premium or credit received by the investor when they sold the spread. Using the same example, we get:

Short 1 April feeder cattle 80 call at .08

Long 1 April feeder cattle 90 call at .02

The net premium received by the investor is 6 cents per pound or $3,000 for the entire position, found as follows:

.06 ´ 50,000 pounds = $3,000

This amount represents the investor's maximum gain. The investor will realize their maximum gain if both options expire.

MAXIMUM LOSS BEAR CALL SPREAD

The investor's maximum loss on a bear call spread has been limited because they bought the call with the higher strike price. If the investor was only short a naked call, their maximum loss would be unlimited. To determine the maximum loss on a bear call spread, use the following formula:

difference in the strike price – net premium received

Using the same example, we get:

Short 1 April feeder cattle 80 call at .08

Long 1 April feeder cattle 90 call at .02

10 – 6 = 4

The investor's maximum loss is 4 cents per pound or $2,000 for the entire position, found as follows:

.04 × 50,000 pounds = $2,000

The investor will realize their maximum loss if both options are exercised.

DETERMINING THE BREAKEVEN FOR A BEAR CALL SPREAD

To determine where the futures contract has to be at expiration for the investor to break even, use the following formula:

lower strike price + net premium

Using the same example, we get:

Short 1 April feeder cattle 80 call at .08

Long 1 April feeder cattle 90 call at .02

$80 + 6 = 86$

If at expiration, April feeder cattle is at 86 cents per pound, the investor will break even on the position, excluding transaction costs. If the futures contract is higher than 86 cents per pound, the investor will lose money. If it is lower than 86 cents per pound, the investor will make money.

SPREAD PREMIUMS BEAR CALL SPREAD

An investor who has established a bear call spread has sold the spread and received a net premium or credit to establish the position. The investor will realize a profit on the spread if the difference in the premiums decreases or narrows. Let's look at our example again:

Short 1 April feeder cattle 80 call at .08

Long 1 April feeder cattle 90 call at .02

The difference between the premiums on the short April 80 call and the long April 90 call is 6 cents. If the difference in the value of the premiums decreases or narrows, the investor will make money. Let's look at the value of the same spread at expiration, given different closing prices for April feeder cattle.

	Opened at	Cattle at 87	Cattle at 92	Cattle at 79
Short 1 April feeder cattle 80 call	.08	7	12	0
Long 1 April feeder cattle 90 call	.02	0	2	0
Difference	.06	7	10	0
Profit/Loss	N/A	($500)	($2,000)	$3,000

Let's compare a bull call spread with a bear call spread.

Position	Max Gain	Max Loss	Breakeven	At Expiration
Bull call spread	Difference in strike prices – premium paid	Net premium paid	Lower strike price + premium	Profitable if spread widens

Position	Max Gain	Max Loss	Breakeven	At Expiration
Bear call spread	Net premium received	Difference in strike prices – premium received	Lower strike price + premium	Profitable if spread narrows

BEAR PUT SPREADS/DEBIT PUT SPREADS

An investor wishing to profit from a decline in the price of a futures contract may establish a bear put spread, also known as a debit put spread. A bear put spread will always be a debit put spread because the right to sell a futures contract at a higher price is always going to be worth more than the right to sell the same futures contract at a lower price for the same amount of time. To establish a debit put spread, the investor will purchase the put with the higher strike price and sell the put with the lower strike price. By selling the put with the lower strike price, the investor has reduced their maximum loss by the amount of the premium received.

The investor has also limited their maximum gain, and any profit from the decline in the price of the futures contract past the lower put's strike price will belong to the investor who purchased the put. Before an investor establishes a bear put spread, they must determine:

- Their maximum gain.
- Their maximum loss.
- Their breakeven.

MAXIMUM GAIN BEAR PUT SPREAD/DEBIT PUT SPREAD

The maximum gain for an investor who has established a bear put spread is found by using the following formula:

difference in the strike prices – net premium paid

Changing our feeder cattle example to puts, we get:

Long 1 April feeder cattle 90 put at .08

Short 1 April feeder cattle 80 put at .02

10 – 6 = 4

The investor's maximum gain is 4 cents per pound or $2,000 (4 cents × 50,000 pounds) for the entire position. The investor will realize their maximum gain if both options are exercised.

MAXIMUM LOSS BEAR PUT SPREAD

An investor who is long a bear put spread has a maximum loss equal to the amount of the net premium paid for the spread. An investor will realize their maximum loss if both options expire worthless.

DETERMINING THE BREAKEVEN FOR A BEAR PUT SPREAD

To determine an investor's breakeven point on a bear put spread, use the following formula:

higher strike price – net premium paid

Using the same example, we get:

Long 1 April feeder cattle 90 put at .08

Short 1 April feeder cattle 80 put at .02

90 – 6 = 84

April feeder cattle would have to fall to 84 cents per pound by expiration for the investor to break even. If at expiration, April feeder cattle has fallen below 84 cents, the investor will make money. At any point above 84 cents, the investor will lose money.

SPREAD PREMIUMS BEAR PUT SPREAD

An investor who has established a bear put spread has bought the spread and paid a net premium to establish the position. The investor will realize a profit on the spread if the difference in the premiums increases or widens. Let's look at our example again:

Long 1 April feeder cattle 90 put at .08

Short 1 April feeder cattle 80 put at .02

The difference between the premium on the long April 90 put and the short April 80 put is 6 cents. If the difference in the value of the premiums increases or widens, the investor will make money. Let's look at the value of the same spread at expiration, given different closing prices for April feeder cattle.

	Opened at	Cattle at 83	Cattle at 88	Cattle at 79
Long 1 April feeder cattle 90 put	.08	7	2	11
Short 1 April feeder cattle 80 put	.02	0	0	1
Difference	.06	7	2	10
Profit/Loss	N/A	$500	($2,000)	$2,000

BULL PUT SPREADS/CREDIT PUT SPREADS

An investor wishing to profit from a rise in the price of a futures contract may establish a bull put spread, also known as a credit put spread. A bull put spread will always be a credit put spread because the right to sell a futures contract at a higher price is always going to be worth more than the right to sell the same futures contract at a lower price for the same amount of time. To establish a bull put spread or credit put spread, the investor would sell the put with the higher strike price and purchase the put with the lower strike price. An investor could profit from a rise in the price of the futures contract by establishing a bull put spread as follows:

Short 1 April feeder cattle 90 put at .08

Long 1 April feeder cattle 80 put at .02

Before an investor establishes a bull put spread, they need to determine:

- Their maximum gain.
- Their maximum loss.
- Their breakeven.

MAXIMUM GAIN BULL PUT SPREAD

The maximum gain for a bull put spread is equal to the credit received by the investor when they sold the spread. Using the same example, we get:

Short 1 April feeder cattle 90 put at .08

Long 1 April feeder cattle 80 put at .02

The investor received a net credit of 6 cents per pound or $3,000 for the entire position, found as follows:

$.06 \times 50,000$ pounds $= \$3,000$

The investor will realize their maximum gain if both options expire.

MAXIMUM LOSS BULL PUT SPREAD

The maximum loss on a bull put spread is found by using the following formula:

difference in the strike prices − net premium received

Short 1 April feeder cattle 90 put at .08

Long 1 April feeder cattle 80 put at .02

Using the same example, we get:

$10 - 6 = 4$

The investor's maximum loss is 4 cents per pound or $2,000, found as follows:

$.04 \times 50,000 = \$2,000$

The investor will realize their maximum loss if both options are exercised.

DETERMINING THE BREAKEVEN FOR A BULL PUT SPREAD

To determine an investor's breakeven point on a bull put spread, use the following formula:

higher strike price – net premium received

Short 1 April feeder cattle 90 put at .08

Long 1 April feeder cattle 80 put at .02

Using the same example, we get:

90 - 6 = 84

April feeder cattle could to fall to 84 cents per pound by expiration and the investor would still break even. If at expiration April feeder cattle is above 84, the investors will make money. At any point below 84, the investor will lose money.

SPREAD PREMIUMS BULL PUT SPREAD

An investor who has established a bull put spread has sold the spread and received a net premium to establish the position. The investor will realize a profit on the spread if the difference in the premiums decreases or narrows. Let's look at our example again:

Short 1 April feeder cattle 90 put at .08

Long 1 April feeder cattle 80 put at .02

The difference between the premium on the short April 90 put and the long April 80 put is 6 cents. If the difference in the value of the premiums decreases or narrows, the investor will make money. Let's look at the value of the same spread at expiration, given different closing prices for April feeder cattle.

	Opened at	Cattle at 87	Cattle at 92	Cattle at 79
Long 1 April feeder cattle 90 put	.08	3	0	11
Short 1 April feeder cattle 80 put	.02	0	0	1
Difference	.06	3	0	10
Profit/Loss	N/A	$1,500	$3,000	($2,000)

Let's compare a bear put spread with a bull put spread.

	Max Gain	Max Loss	Breakeven	At Expiration
Bear put spread	Difference in strike prices – premium paid	Net premium paid	Higher strike price – premium	Profitable if spread widens
Bull put spread	Net premium received	Difference in strike prices – premium received	Higher strike price – premium	Profitable if spread narrows

SYNTHETIC RISK AND REWARD

Understanding the risk and reward potential of any position can substantially help an investor realize their investment objectives. Certain futures and option positions have substantially similar risk and reward profiles and, as a result, have come to be known as synthetics. The following chart lists various positions and their synthetic equivalents.

Position	Synthetic
Long futures	Long call + short put
Short futures	Short call + long put
Long call	Long futures + long put
Short call	Short futures + short put
Long put	Short futures + long call
Short put	Long futures + short call

LONG FUTURES SHORT CALLS/COVERED CALLS

An investor who is long futures can receive some partial downside protection and generate some additional income by selling calls against the futures they own. The investor will receive downside protection or will hedge their position by the amount of the premium received from the sale of the calls. While the investor will receive partial downside protection, they will also give up any appreciation potential above the call's strike price.

LONG FUTURES LONG PUTS/MARRIED PUTS

An investor who is long futures and wishes to protect the position from downside risk will receive the most protection by purchasing a protective put. By purchasing the put, the investor has locked in or set a minimum sale price that they will receive in the event the futures decline for the life of the put. The minimum sale price in this case is equal to the strike price of the put. Long puts can be used with long futures to guard against a loss or to protect an unrealized profit. However by purchasing the put, the investor has increased their breakeven point by the amount of the premium they paid to purchase the put.

SHORT FUTURES LONG CALLS

An investor who sells futures short believes that they can profit from a fall in the futures price by selling it high and repurchasing it cheaper. An investor who has sold futures short is subject to an unlimited loss if the futures price should begin to rise. Once again there is no limit to how high the price of a futures contract may rise. An investor who has sold futures short would receive the most protection by purchasing a call. A long call could be used to guard against a loss or to protect a profit on a short futures position. By purchasing the call, the investor has set the maximum price that they will have to pay to repurchase the futures for the life of the option.

SHORT FUTURES SHORT PUTS

An investor who has sold futures short can receive some protection and generate premium income by selling puts against their short futures position. Selling puts against a short futures position will only partially hedge the unlimited upside risk associated with any short sale of futures. Additionally, the investor, in exchange for the premium received for the sale of the put, has further limited their maximum gain.

CONVERSIONS AND REVERSALS

There are two arbitrage positions you may be required to identify on your exam. These positions are known as conversions and reversals. These positions seek to lock in a risk-free profit as a result of pricing inefficiencies in the option market. With a conversion the investor will go long the futures contract, long the put and short the call. A reversal is established by going short the futures contract, long the call and short the put. for your exam you would most likely only be required to identify how the position is established.

DELTA

Delta is a measure of an option's price change in relation to a price change in the underlying contract. All options do not change in price by the same amount when the price of the underlying futures contract changes.

Options that are deep in the money have deltas that are close to one.

When an option's delta is 1 (100%), a change in the price of the underlying futures contract will be reflected 100% in the change in the price of the deep in the money option. At the money options have deltas that are approximately 50, so that 50% of the change in price of the futures contract will be reflected in the price change of the option. The further the option is out of the money, the lower its delta. If a trader was seeking to protect a futures position using an option with a delta of 50 it would take 2 options to fully hedge the futures contract. To determine how many options would be needed to effectively hedge a futures contract, divide the delta into 100. If a trader wanted to hedge a long futures position using out of the money puts with a delta of 25, it would take four contracts to hedge the position as follows $100 \div 25 = 4$. To determine how much an option's premium would change given a delta and a change in the underlying futures contract, multiply the price change in the futures contract by the delta. If the price of gold increased by $10, an at the money gold call option with a delta of 50 would increase by 50% of that amount or by $5, found as follows: $10 $\times .5 = \$5$.

USING A T CHART TO EVALUATE OPTION POSITIONS

Many option positions can be evaluated by simply analyzing the flow of funds into or out of the investor's account. To analyze option positions, use the following T chart:

Debit	Credit

A debit in the customer's account results in an outflow of funds, whereas a credit results in an inflow of funds.

Let's analyze several option positions using the T chart. An investor buys 1 June Crude 50 call at 5

Debit	Credit
5	

The purchase of the call results in a net debit equal to the amount of the premium paid by the investor. To determine the investor's breakeven, add the price that the investor would have to pay for the futures contract if the investor exercised the call option. This will always be equal to the call's strike price. If the investor exercised the option, the flow of funds would look as follows:

Debit	Credit
5	
50	

55

This investor would breakeven at expiration if June crude was at 55. Let's look at the flow of funds for an investor who buys a put.

An investor purchases 1 June gold 1170 put at 4

Debit	Credit
4	

The purchase of the put results in a net debit equal to the amount of the premium that the investor paid for the option. To determine the investor's breakeven, enter the price that the investor would receive from exercising the put as a credit. This will always be equal to the put's strike price. Remember that the owner of the put will sell the futures contract if the option is exercised and the sale of futures contract will always result in a credit into the account. If the investor exercised the option, the flow of funds will look as follows:

Debit	Credit
4	1170

1166

The difference between the debit and credit will equal the investor's breakeven. Let's look at the flow of funds for an investor who is long a futures contract and short a call. An investor is long 1 March crude at 50 and short 1 March crude 55 call at 3.

Debit	Credit
50	3

47

The investor has paid 50 for the futures contract and received 3 from the sale of the call; therefore, the investor's net outlay of cash is 47, and this will be the breakeven. That is to say that the futures contract could fall to 47 and the investor would still breakeven. To determine the investor's maximum gain, enter the sales proceeds from the sale of the futures contract in the credit column. This will be equal to the strike price of the option if the option was exercised against the investor and the futures contract was called away.

Debit	Credit
50	3
	55

8

Let's look at the flow of funds for an investor who is long futures contract and long a put.

An investor is long 1 March wheat at 420 and long 1 March wheat 400 put at .20

Debit	Credit
420	
.20	

440

Because the investor has purchased both the futures contract and the protective put, March wheat must rise to 440 in order for the investor to breakeven. The investor's maximum loss will be realized if March wheat falls and the put has to be exercised. To determine the maximum loss, enter the sales proceeds from the exercise of the put in the credit column.

Debit	Credit
4.20	400
.20	

.40

The investor's maximum loss will be 40 cents per bushel.

Let's look at the flow of funds for an investor who is short a futures contract and long a call.

An investor is short 1 December Silver at 19.10 and is long 1December silver 20 call at .30. The flow of funds will look as follows:

Debit	Credit
	19.10
.30	

18.80

December silver would have to fall to 18.80 in order for the investor to break even. The investor will realize the maximum possible loss if silver rises and has to exercise the call to close out the position. The flow of funds in that case will look as follows:

Debit	Credit
.30	19.10
20	

1.20

If the investor has to repurchase the silver contract at 20, the investor would realize the maximum loss of $1.20 per ounce.

Let's look at the flow of funds for an investor who is short futures contract and short a put.

An investor is short 1December crude at 43 and short 1 December crude 40 put at 2. The flow of funds will look as follows:

Debit	Credit
	43
	2

45

December crude could rise to 45 and the investor would still breakeven.

If crude falls and the futures contract is put to the investor at the strike price of the short put, the flow of fund will be as follows:

Debit	Credit
40	43
	2

5

If the futures contract is put to the investor at 40, the investor will realize the maximum profit of $5 per barrel.

The T chart is also effective in analyzing positions created from multiple-option positions, such as straddles and spreads. Let's look at the flow of funds for a long straddle.

An investor is long 1 October gold 1170 call at 4 and long 1 October gold 1170 put at 2:

Debit	Credit
4	
2	

6

The investor's maximum loss is the net debit, or $6 per ounce. Remember that a straddle has two breakevens: one for the call side and one for the put side. The investor in this case will breakeven at 1176 on the call side and 1164 on the put side. If the investor was short the straddle, the premiums would have been entered on the credit side of the chart, and that would represent the investor's maximum gain.

Spreads are created by the simultaneous purchase and sale of two options of the same type on the same underlying contract that differ in strike price,

expiration month, or both. Because the investor is purchasing and selling options, the T chart will have entries in both the debit and credit columns. Let's look at the flow of funds for a bull call spread.

An investor establishes the following position:

Long 1 March corn 300 call at .20
Short 1 March corn 400 call at .10

Debit	Credit
.2	.1

.10

The investor's maximum loss is 10 cents per bushel because that was the net debit in the account. If the investor established a bear call spread by being short this spread, the position would have resulted in a net credit in the account of 10 centers per bushel, and that would be the investor's maximum gain.

The T chart can be used to help determine:

Maximum gain, maximum loss, breakeven for all option positions.

SPREADING FUTURES CONTRACTS

Sophisticated investors will often seek out opportunities to earn a profit by taking advantage of price inefficiencies that exist between the prices of 2 futures contracts by establishing a spread. A spread using futures contracts can be established on the same commodity using different contract months, very similar to a calendar spread in options. This type of spread is known as an intramarket or interdelivery spread and could be established as follows:

Long 1 October gold

Short 1 August gold

With most commodities, when an investor establishes an intra commodity or inter delivery spread, the investor's market sentiment is expressed by the position taken in the front month. If the investor is short the front-month and long the deferred month, the investor is bearish on the commodity. If the investor is long the front month and short the deferred month, the investor is bullish on the commodity. However, for spreads established in financial and currency futures, the Investor's market sentiment is expressed by the position taken in the deferred month.

Investors may find price discrepancies between contracts for the same commodity trading on different exchanges. As a result, the investor may take a long position in the contract on one exchange and take a short position in the contract trading on the other exchange. This type of spread is known as an intermarket spread and could be established as follows:

Buy October gold on the CME

Sell October gold on COMEX

Futures contracts that trade on different exchanges may not be used to offset each other through a journal entry as these are deemed to be different contracts. However, contracts that trade side by side on the CME Globex platform and on the CME floor are deemed to be interchangeable. Additionally, a futures contract traded on the Intercontinental Exchange (ICE) in London is interchangeable with a futures Contract traded on The Exchange in New York.

A product spread may be established in futures contracts by taking a position in the raw commodity and a simultaneous opposite position in the refined or derivative product. This is effective when the price of one of the components of the spread is very high or low relative to the historical price spread between the futures contracts. One popular product spread is the *crack* spread. The crack spread may be used by refiners to hedge a future purchase of crude oil and to hedge a future sale of the refined products it produces. A crack spread is established by taking a long position in crude oil and an opposite short position in refined products, which are RBOB gasoline and heating oil. A crack spread could be established as follows:

Buy 1 December crude

Sell 1 December RBOB gasoline

Sell 1 December heating oil

A reverse crack spread would be established by going long the refined product and short the raw commodity as follows:

Sell 1 December crude

Buy 1 December RBOB gasoline

Buy 1 December heating oil

Another popular product spread is known as the crush spread. The crush spread is often used by bean crushers who purchase soybeans and through the process of crushing create the refined products which are soybean meal and soybean oil. The crush spread may be used by bean crushers to hedge the purchase of the raw input soybeans and to hedge the latter sale of the soybean meal and soybean oil. The crush spread would be established as follows:

Buy June soybeans

Sell June soybean meal

Sell June soybean oil

Bean crushers operate based on the gross processing margin of the crush. The gross processing margin is the difference between the cost of one bushel of beans and the value of the refined soybean meal and oil produced from the bushel. If the gross processing margin is positive the business of crushing beans is profitable. The gross processing margin only takes into consideration the price of the raw soybeans and the value of the refined products. The overhead and other expenses of the crusher's business are not taken into consideration for the gross processing margin.

The reverse crush spread may be established by speculators who feel that the gross processing margin will decline and may profit from business conditions that hurt the crushers. A reverse crush would be established as follows:

Sell June soybeans

Buy June soybean meal

Buy June soybean oil

One more product spread that may be established to hedge business risks of a cattle grower would be a spread in cattle futures. A cattle grower purchases feeder cattle to raise until they have fully matured into live cattle that are ready for processing by the meat industry. A cattle grower may establish a futures spread to hedge business risks by purchasing feeder cattle futures to hedge the future purchase of feeder cattle and by selling live cattle futures to hedge the latter sale of cattle ready for processing.

Intercommodity spreads can be established by taking a long position in one commodity and an opposite short position in a different commodity. The commodities may be related products, substitute products, or have historical price relationships. Gold has historically traded in a multiple range over the price of silver. If the price of gold appreciated past the normal multiple of the price of silver, a spread could be established as follows:

Sell 1 October gold

Buy 2 October silver

Spread orders are entered as one order with two legs and are established for a net credit or net debit. Spread orders may be entered as either market orders or as limit orders. Spread positions in futures contracts may be established as debit or credit spreads. If the more expensive contract or leg is purchased, the position is a debit spread. If the more expensive contract or leg is sold, it is a credit spread. If the investor established a debit spread, the spread will be profitable if the difference between the premiums widens. If the spread is established as a credit spread, it will become profitable if the difference between the premiums narrows.

SPREADING TREASURY FUTURES

A popular spread using Treasury futures is an intermaturity spread. This spread involves establishing a position in T-bill futures while simultaneously establishing an opposite position in T-bond futures. When establishing a spread of this type it is important to remember that the contract size for the underlying instruments varies greatly. The T-bill contract covers a par value of $1 million, while the T-bond contract covers a par value of $100,000. An investor who is looking to establish a dollar weighted spread must establish the spread as a 1:10 spread. That is to say that for each T-bill contract position opened the investor would have to establish an opposite position in 10 T-bond futures. As interest rates change the price of the longer term treasury bond will move more in price than the T-bill. Therefore if an investor felt interest rates were going to fall the investor would sell bills and buy bonds. If the investor felt that rates were going to increase the investor would buy bills and sell bonds. An investor could also establish an intermaturity spread as a hedge using bill and bond futures based on the contract size and the maturity. Because the T-bill contract covers a par value of $1 million based on a 3-month treasury bill, and the bond contract is based on a par value of $100,000, the hedge must be established at a 4:1 ratio based on the par value. For every two bill contracts established the investor must establish an off-setting position in five T-bond contracts. This would result in a bill position based on $2,000,000 in par value against a bond position of $500,000. Once established if both long and short term rates change by the same amount the change in the aggregate price of each position should be approximately equal. The final type of spread you may see involving treasury futures is created by using offsetting positions in 10 year treasury notes and 30 year bonds, This is known as the NOB spread. Short for notes over bonds. An investor who wanted to profit from a change in the yield curve may establish a NOB spread to profit from the change. An investor who felt that the yield curve was going to steepen would sell the bond futures contract and purchase the note futures contract. As long-term interest rates increase as a result of the steepening yield curve, the price of the treasury bond contract would fall more than the price of the note contract. Investors who feel that the yield curve will flatten, would go long the bond contract and short the note contract. As long-term interest rates fall as a result of the flattening yield curve, the price of the bond contract would increase by more than the price of the note contract. The NOB spread is traditionally established at a ratio of 2 note contracts for every offsetting bond contract.

THE TED SPREAD

The TED spread is created by establishing a position in both Treasury bill futures and Eurodollar futures. A Eurodollar is a US dollar held in an interest bearing account in any country outside of the US. The TED spread is used by investors to speculate on or to hedge against changes in interest rates or credit conditions. Treasury bills are considered to be AAA rated credit and Eurodollars are deemed to be AA rated credit. As such, the interest rate on the Eurodollars should be slightly higher than the corresponding interest rate on the Treasury bills. Investors who are concerned about a rise in interest rates or a deterioration of credit would establish a TED spread by going long Treasury bill futures and short Eurodollar futures. As interest rates increase, the value of the Eurodollar contract should fall by more than the Treasury bill contract and the spread between the two would widen. Going long the TED spread can also be seen as being bearish on the economy. Alternatively, investors who believe that interest rates will fall or that credit conditions will improve would go short the TED spread and would sell Treasury bill futures and buy Eurodollars. In this case, as interest rates fall or credit improves, the value of the long Eurodollar contract should increase by more than the value of the short Treasury bill contract, causing the spread to narrow. Investors who sell the TED spread are considered to be bullish on the economy.

TAKE**NOTE!**

The margin requirement for spread positions is typically lower than the speculative margin requirement due to the fact that spreads in futures contracts are effectively hedging each other. When one contract in the spread becomes the front month contract the CME group requires the full margin requirement for that contract.

Pretest

1. When silver is trading at 18.34 an ounce, an investor has established the following option position:

   Long 5 December silver 18 call at 1.25

   The investor will break even at expiration if silver is trading at:
   a. 19.25.
   b. 25.25.
   c. 17.25.
   d. 19.50.

2. When an investor sells a put option to open with no other option or futures position in the account, the investor's maximum loss is unlimited.

   True
   False

3. A wheat trader is looking at the prices for near-term call options on July wheat futures. The July wheat contract is trading at 5.14 per bushel with cash wheat trading in the spot market at 5.10. The 5 calls on July wheat are trading at 17 cents. The calls have time value of:
   a. 7 cents.
   b. 3 cents.
   c. 14 cents.
   d. 10 cents.

4. Options on Treasury futures are quoted in:
   a. 32nds of 1% of $1,000,000.
   b. 64ths of 1% of $1,000,000.
   c. 32nds of 1% of $100,000.
   d. 64ths of 1% of $100,000.

5. A long straddle is the simultaneous purchase of a call and a put on the same futures contract with the same strike price and expiration month.

   True
   False

6. The maximum gain on a short straddle is:
   a. Unlimited.
   b. The total premium received.
   c. The total premium paid.
   d. The difference between the premiums.

7. A wheat trader establishes the following position:

   Long 1 March wheat 570 put

   Short 1 March wheat 550 put
   Which of the following are true?
   I. The position is a vertical spread.
   II. The investor believes that wheat will increase in price.
   III. This is a credit spread.
   IV. This is a debit spread.
   a. II and III
   b. I and IV
   c. I and II
   d. IV only

8. A diagonal spread consists of 1 long call option and 1 short put option or 1 long put option and 1 short call option on the same futures contract.
   True
   False

9. An investor buys 2 April feeder cattle 80 calls at .07 when April feeder cattle is trading at 82. With each futures contract covering 50,000 pounds, what was the total premium paid by the investor for the April 80 calls?
   a. $3,500
   b. $2,000
   c. $1,000
   d. $7,000

10. An investor who is long October gold could establish a product spread be executing which of the following orders?
    a. Buy October silver.
    b. Sell September corn.
    c. Sell December platinum.
    d. Buy October copper.

CFTC & NFA and Regulations

INTRODUCTION

Federal commodities laws, as well as industry and exchange regulations, have been enacted to ensure that all commodities industry participants adhere to a high standard of just and equitable trade practices. In this chapter, we will review the rules and regulations governing the commodities futures and options industry, as well as the registration requirements for firms and agents.

THE COMMODITY EXCHANGE ACT OF 1936

The Commodity Exchange Act of 1936 replaced the Grain Futures Act of 1922 and required that any transaction in commodity futures or commodity futures options take place on the floor of an exchange and not in the over-the-counter or OTC market. In 1975 the Commodity Exchange Act was amended and the Commodity Futures Trading Commission or CFTC was created by Congress to oversee the trading in all futures contracts. The CFTC is a direct government agency and is the ultimate regulator in the commodity futures industry. The CFTC is not a self-regulatory organization (SRO). A self-regulatory organization is one that regulates its own members such as the Chicago Mercantile Exchange (CME) or the National Futures Association (NFA). The CFTC has five commissioners who are appointed by the president, and each must be approved by Congress. The CFTC has the ultimate authority to oversee all industry participants and has exclusive jurisdiction over disciplinary actions involving all commodity exchanges and floor brokers. The CFTC is designed to ensure and promote ethical trading and to guard against price manipulation and the use of false statements in the futures industry. The terms of all futures and option contracts set by futures exchanges must be approved by the CFTC. Individuals who are employed by the CFTC are prohibited from trading futures contracts. The CFTC may subpoena records without a court order and may go to court to seek a restraining order against someone who is found to have violated the rules of the Commodity Exchange Act. If the CFTC finds that its rules have been violated it may:

- Suspend the firm or individual.
- Revoke the registration of a firm or individual.
- Suspend or revoke trading privileges.
- Fine a maximum amount of $140,000 per violation or three times the amount of the gain.

A criminal violation of the Commodity Exchange Act carries a penalty of up to 10 years in prison and a fine up to $1,00,000 in addition to the suspension or revocation of registration.

THE NATIONAL FUTURES ASSOCIATION

The National Futures Association (NFA) is the SRO for the futures industry. Its main areas of focus are:

- To ensure ethical behavior
- To ensure individuals meet minimum training and knowledge standards
- To ensure firms meet minimum financial standards
- To conduct unannounced spot audits of members
- To conduct full-scope member audits every 24 months
- To review registrations
- To provide a forum for dispute resolution

Any individual or organization that intends to transact futures business with members of the investing public must become registered with the National Futures Association (NFA). NFA members may only deal with other NFA members on a preferential basis and share commissions. Any non-NFA member or suspended member must be treated as a member of the general public. Individuals who are going to be registered as associated persons ask their employing firm's security manager to file the application with the NFA through the Online Registration System (ORS). Once the registration process has begun, the individual will be assigned an NFA ID number that will be used by them throughout their career in the futures industry. An associated person (AP) is an individual who solicits orders, customers, or customer funds or who supervises persons engaged in these activities on behalf of a futures commission merchant (FCM), introducing broker (IB), commodity trading adviser (CTA), or commodity pool operator (CPO). Effectively an AP is anyone who is a salesperson or who supervises salespersons. An associated person may be registered simultaneously with more than one firm provided both firms agree to the dual registration. Each firm is also required to register with the NFA. The type of NFA registration will depend upon the type of business conducted by the firm. Firms may register as:

Futures Commission Merchants (FCM).

Introducing Brokers (IB).

Commodity Pool Operators (CPO).

Commodity Trading Advisers (CTA).

FUTURES COMMISSION MERCHANT

A futures commission merchant (FCM) is a firm that transacts futures business and executes orders for customer accounts. In addition to executing customer orders, a futures commission merchant may also hold customer funds as margin or to guarantee customer futures contracts. An FCM must have minimum net capital of at least $1,000,000 and file statements of financial condition each month within 17 days of the end of the month. An FCM that maintains the accounts of its customers and holds their cash and securities is known as a *clearing firm* or a clearing member and are members of the clearing corp. Not all FCMs maintain the physical possession of the customers' cash and securities. A merchant may find it easier to have another futures commission merchant provide the clearing and custodial functions for its customers' accounts. The FCM may choose to clear their trades on a fully disclosed basis or through an omnibus account maintained at the clearing firm. If a firm clears all of their transactions on a fully disclosed basis, all customer confirmations and statements will be sent by the clearing member. If the FCM clears its trades on an omnibus basis, all transactions are cleared through one account and the clearing member does not know for whom the trade was executed. The introducing member is required to send customer confirmations and statements if they clear through an omnibus account. All FCMs must inspect its branch offices annually as well as the offices of any introducing broker guaranteed by the FCM.

INTRODUCING BROKER

An introducing broker is an individual or organization that solicits or accepts customer orders for futures and options on futures. The introducing broker may not accept checks made out in its own name. The IB forwards all cash and securities to the futures commission merchant (FCM) for deposit into the customers' accounts. All funds must be deposited into a qualified bank account entitled "segregated customer funds" on the day of receipt. The introducing broker may make the deposit directly into the segregated account of the FCM so long as the IB has on file the written authorization to do so. This authorization must be maintained by the IB and the account must only allow withdrawals by the FCM. This is known as a one-way account. The clearing merchant sends the customers' statements and confirmations to the introducing broker's customers and all accounts are carried by the clearing FCM on a fully disclosed basis. All introducing brokers must maintain minimum net capital of at least $45,000. If the IB does not or cannot maintain this level of net capital it may have its solvency guaranteed by the FCM it introduces its customer accounts to. In order to operate as a guaranteed IB, the firm must have a written guarantee agreement from the FCM and the IB may only be guaranteed by one FCM. The guarantee agreement may be open ended and in force until terminated in writing. An IB may introduce trades to more than one FCM, but if the IB is a guaranteed introducing broker (GIB), most FCMs that guarantee introducing brokers will require that the IB introduce all trades exclusively as a condition of the guarantee. Once the guarantee is in place the FCM is responsible for all of the activities of the IB and can be found criminally and civilly liable for the actions of the IB.

 TAKE**NOTE!**

An FCM may guarantee an unlimited number of IBs as part of its business as long as it has the required net capital to do so. An Introducing broker however, may only be guaranteed by one FCM.

COMMODITY POOL OPERATOR

A Commodity Pool Operator (CPO) is an organization which invests money contributed by a group of participants to a single account for the purpose of investing the money in futures contracts, options on futures, retail off-exchange forex contracts or swaps, or to invest in another commodity pool. The CPO must operate each pool as a single commodity pool if it operates more than one commodity pool. Customer contributions to the pool must be made out in the name of the specific commodity pool. Investors in the commodity pool will own an interest in the specific pool. Registration as a CPO is required for any CPO who

- Manages a pool or a group of pools with more than $400,000 in total assets in all pools

Or

- Manages a pool with more than 15 investors, excluding the operator of the pool and their immediate family

EXAMPLE XYZ CPO has two pools, one that invests in metals and one that invests in agricultural products. Each pool has $350,000 invested in it by six investors. XYZ as the operator must register as a CPO because the total amount invested in the two pools is $700,000 and is greater than the $400,000 threshold.

Operators are exempt from registering as a CPO if the total amount invested in all pools is less than $400,000 and the total number of investors in any one pool does not exceed 15 investors. Operators of commodity investment clubs are also exempt from registration as a CPO so long as:

- The operator does not receive compensation for operating the club.
- The operator manages only one commodity pool at any one time.
- The operator does not advertise the club.

The operator of the investment club is entitled to be reimbursed for expenses incurred during the course of operating the club.

The operator of any commodity pool or club who is exempt from registration must file a notice with the NFA citing the reasons why the pool or club is exempt from registering as a CPO. A copy of this notice must be sent to each of the participants.

Participants in commodity pools must get monthly statements if the value of the pool is greater than $500,000. If the value of the pool is $500,000 or less, the participants must get quarterly statements. All statements must show the changes in the net asset value (NAV) of the pool inclusive of all fees and charges. Statements and value computations must be calculated using generally accepted account principles (GAAP). A CPO that charges upfront fees and/or passes along the expenses of formation or other expenses to investors must disclose the costs and fees prominently on the front cover of the CPO's disclosure document.

COMMODITY TRADING ADVISER

A commodity trading adviser (CTA) is an individual or business who, for compensation or profit, advises others on trading futures contracts or options on futures contracts. A CTA is also someone who advises as to the value of futures contracts, options on futures, retail off-exchange forex contracts, or swaps. The definition of providing advice includes exercising trading authority over a customer's account as well as giving advice based upon knowledge of a customer's commodity account, commodity trading activity, or practices. A CTA may not accept customer funds and may not carry customer accounts. Each CTA is required to disclose to clients the identity of the FCM who will carry the customers' account and if the CTA has any affiliation with the FCM. All customer accounts are carried at an FCM on a fully disclosed basis and the FCM is required to send out customer confirmations and statements. All advisers must register as a CTA unless:

- It has advised 15 or fewer clients in the last 12 months and does not hold itself out to the public as a commodity trading adviser.
- It is a commodity pool operator and only advises its own pools.
- It is a publisher.
- It is an investment club.
- Individuals who transact business or advise others in the cash market only.
- Anyone who is registered as an AP, CPO, or floor broker and the advice given is incidental to their registered function.

RISK DISCLOSURE DOCUMENTS

Both commodity pool operators (CPO) and commodity trading advisers (CTA) must prepare risk disclosure documents to be filed with the NFA and to be given to all prospective investors. These documents must be filed with the NFA 21 days prior to being given to any potential investors. The effective date must be published on the front cover and the effective date may be no earlier than 21 days from the date the documents were filed with the NFA. The financial information filed must be current and may be no more than 3 months old. The documents must be updated every 9 months. Disclosure Documents ("Documents") for CTAs must include the following information:

Cover Page

The cover page of the Document must prominently include the Cautionary Statement below. Prominently means displayed in CAPITAL letters and in boldface type.

THE COMMODITY FUTURES TRADING COMMISSION HAS NOT PASSED UPON THE MERITS OF PARTICIPATING IN THIS TRADING PROGRAM NOR HAS THE COMMISSION PASSED ON THE ADEQUACY OR ACCURACY OF THIS DIS-

CLOSURE DOCUMENT.

Risk Disclosure Statement

The following Risk Disclosure Statement must be prominently displayed immediately after the cover page of the Document.

RISK DISCLOSURE STATEMENT

THE RISK OF LOSS IN TRADING COMMODITY INTERESTS CAN BE SUBSTANTIAL. YOU SHOULD THEREFORE CAREFULLY CONSIDER WHETHER SUCH TRADING IS SUITABLE FOR YOU IN LIGHT OF YOUR FINANCIAL CONDITION. IN CONSIDERING WHETHER TO TRADE OR TO AUTHORIZE SOMEONE ELSE TO TRADE FOR YOU, YOU SHOULD BE AWARE OF THE FOLLOWING:

IF YOU PURCHASE A COMMODITY OPTION YOU MAY SUSTAIN A TOTAL LOSS OF THE PREMIUM AND OF ALL TRANSACTION COSTS.

IF YOU PURCHASE OR SELL A COMMODITY FUTURES CONTRACT OR SELL A COMMODITY OPTION OR ENGAGE IN OFF-EXCHANGE FOREIGN CURRENCY TRADING YOU MAY SUSTAIN A TOTAL LOSS OF THE INITIAL MARGIN FUNDS OR SECURITY DEPOSIT AND ANY ADDITIONAL FUNDS THAT YOU DEPOSIT WITH YOUR BROKER TO ESTABLISH OR MAINTAIN YOUR POSITION. IF THE MARKET MOVES AGAINST YOUR POSITION, YOU MAY BE CALLED UPON BY YOUR BROKER TO DEPOSIT A SUBSTANTIAL AMOUNT OF ADDITIONAL MARGIN FUNDS, ON SHORT NOTICE, IN ORDER TO MAINTAIN YOUR POSITION. IF YOU DO NOT PROVIDE THE REQUESTED FUNDS WITHIN THE PRESCRIBED TIME, YOUR POSITION MAY BE LIQUIDATED AT A LOSS, AND YOU WILL BE LIABLE FOR ANY RESULTING DEFICIT IN YOUR ACCOUNT.

UNDER CERTAIN MARKET CONDITIONS, YOU MAY FIND IT DIFFICULT OR IMPOSSIBLE TO LIQUIDATE A POSITION. THIS CAN OCCUR, FOR EXAMPLE, WHEN THE MARKET MAKES A "LIMIT MOVE."

THE PLACEMENT OF CONTINGENT ORDERS BY YOU OR YOUR TRADING ADVISER, SUCH AS A "STOP-LOSS" OR "STOP-LIMIT" ORDER, WILL NOT NECESSARILY LIMIT YOUR LOSSES TO THE INTENDED AMOUNTS, SINCE MARKET CONDITIONS

MAY MAKE IT IMPOSSIBLE TO EXECUTE SUCH ORDERS.

A "SPREAD" POSITION MAY NOT BE LESS RISKY THAN A SIMPLE "LONG" OR "SHORT" POSITION.

THE HIGH DEGREE OF LEVERAGE THAT IS OFTEN OBTAINABLE IN COMMODITY INTEREST TRADING CAN WORK AGAINST YOU AS WELL AS FOR YOU. THE USE OF LEVERAGE CAN LEAD TO LARGE LOSSES AS WELL AS GAINS.

IN SOME CASES, MANAGED COMMODITY ACCOUNTS ARE SUBJECT TO SUBSTANTIAL CHARGES FOR MANAGEMENT AND ADVISORY FEES. IT MAY BE NECESSARY FOR THOSE ACCOUNTS THAT ARE SUBJECT TO THESE CHARGES TO MAKE SUBSTANTIAL TRADING PROFITS TO AVOID DEPLETION OR EXHAUSTION OF THEIR ASSETS. THIS DISCLOSURE DOCUMENT CONTAINS, AT PAGE (insert page number), A COMPLETE DESCRIPTION OF EACH FEE TO BE CHARGED TO YOUR ACCOUNT BY THE COMMODITY TRADING ADVISER.

THIS BRIEF STATEMENT CANNOT DISCLOSE ALL THE RISKS AND OTHER SIGNIFICANT ASPECTS OF THE COMMODITY INTEREST MARKETS. YOU SHOULD THEREFORE CAREFULLY STUDY THIS DISCLOSURE DOCUMENT AND COMMODITY INTEREST TRADING BEFORE YOU TRADE, INCLUDING THE DESCRIPTION OF THE PRINCIPAL RISK FACTORS OF THIS INVESTMENT, AT PAGE (insert page number).

If the CTA may trade foreign futures or options contracts on foreign exchanges, the Risk Disclosure Statement must further state the following:

YOU SHOULD ALSO BE AWARE THAT THIS COMMODITY TRADING ADVISER MAY ENGAGE IN TRADING FOREIGN FUTURES OR OPTIONS CONTRACTS. TRANSACTIONS ON MARKETS LOCATED OUTSIDE THE UNITED STATES, INCLUDING MARKETS FORMALLY LINKED TO A UNITED STATES MARKET, MAY BE SUBJECT TO REGULATIONS WHICH OFFER DIFFERENT OR DIMINISHED PROTECTION. FURTHER, UNITED STATES REGULATORY AUTHORITIES MAY BE UNABLE TO COMPEL THE ENFORCEMENT OF THE RULES OF REGULATORY AUTHORITIES OR MARKETS IN NON-UNITED STATES JURISDICTIONS WHERE YOUR TRANSACTIONS MAY BE EFFECTED. BEFORE YOU TRADE YOU SHOULD INQUIRE

ABOUT ANY RULES RELEVANT TO YOUR PARTICULAR CON-TEMPLATED TRANSACTIONS AND ASK THE FIRM WITH WHICH YOU INTEND TO TRADE FOR DETAILS ABOUT THE TYPES OF REDRESS AVAILABLE IN BOTH YOUR LOCAL AND OTHER RELEVANT JURISDICTIONS.

If the CTA may engage in retail forex transactions pursuant to the offered trading program, the Risk Disclosure Statement must further state the following:

ON AN ANNUAL BASIS THE NFA WILL SEND EACH NFA MEMBER FCM RFED, IB, CPO, CTA, AND LTM A BUSINESS PROFILE QUESTIONNAIRE RELATING TO THE MEMBER'S BUSINESS ACTIVITIES. THE MEMBER MUST COMPLETE THE QUESTIONNAIRE AND SUBMIT THE COMPLETED QUESTIONNAIRE ON THE DATE SPECIFIED THEREON. NFA SHALL DEEM THE FAILURE TO FILE THE COMPLETED QUES-TIONNAIRE WITHIN 30 DAYS FOLLOWING SUCH DATE A REQUEST TO WITHDRAW FROM NFA MEMBERSHIP, AND SHALL NOTIFY THE MEMBER ACCORDINGLY.

CPO Risk Disclosure must include the following:

Cover Page
The cover page of the Document must prominently include the Cautionary Statement below. Prominently means displayed in CAPITAL letters and in boldface type.

THE COMMODITY FUTURES TRADING COMMISSION HAS NOT PASSED UPON THE MERITS OF PARTICIPATING IN THIS POOL NOR HAS THE COMMISSION PASSED ON THE ADE-QUACY OR ACCURACY OF THIS DISCLOSURE DOCUMENT.

Risk Disclosure Statement
The applicable Risk Disclosure Statement must be prominently displayed immediately after the cover page of the Document.

If the pool trades commodity interests, the following Risk Disclosure Statement is required.

RISK DISCLOSURE STATEMENT

YOU SHOULD CAREFULLY CONSIDER WHETHER YOUR FINANCIAL CONDITION PERMITS YOU TO PARTICIPATE IN A COMMODITY POOL. IN SO DOING, YOU SHOULD BE AWARE THAT COMMODITY INTEREST TRADING CAN QUICKLY LEAD TO LARGE LOSSES AS WELL AS GAINS. SUCH TRADING LOSSES CAN SHARPLY REDUCE THE NET ASSET VALUE OF THE POOL AND CONSEQUENTLY THE VALUE OF YOUR INTEREST IN THE POOL. IN ADDITION, RESTRICTIONS ON REDEMPTIONS MAY AFFECT YOUR ABILITY TO WITHDRAW YOUR PARTICIPATION IN THE POOL.

FURTHER, COMMODITY POOLS MAY BE SUBJECT TO SUBSTANTIAL CHARGES FOR MANAGEMENT, AND ADVISORY AND BROKERAGE FEES. IT MAY BE NECESSARY FOR THOSE POOLS THAT ARE SUBJECT TO THESE CHARGES TO MAKE SUBSTANTIAL TRADING PROFITS TO AVOID DEPLETION OR EXHAUSTION OF THEIR ASSETS. THIS DISCLOSURE DOCUMENT CONTAINS A COMPLETE DESCRIPTION OF EACH EXPENSE TO BE CHARGED THIS POOL AT PAGE [insert page number] AND A STATEMENT OF THE PERCENTAGE RETURN NECESSARY TO BREAK EVEN, THAT IS, TO RECOVER THE AMOUNT OF YOUR INITIAL INVESTMENT, AT PAGE [insert page number].

THIS BRIEF STATEMENT CANNOT DISCLOSE ALL THE RISKS AND OTHER FACTORS NECESSARY TO EVALUATE YOUR PARTICIPATION IN THIS COMMODITY POOL. THEREFORE, BEFORE YOU DECIDE TO PARTICIPATE IN THIS COMMODITY POOL, YOU SHOULD CAREFULLY STUDY THIS DISCLOSURE DOCUMENT, INCLUDING A DESCRIPTION OF THE PRINCIPAL RISK FACTORS OF THIS INVESTMENT, AT PAGE [insert page number].

If the pool trades foreign futures or options contracts on foreign exchanges, the Risk Disclosure Statement must further state the following:

YOU SHOULD ALSO BE AWARE THAT THIS COMMODITY POOL MAY TRADE FOREIGN FUTURES OR OPTIONS CONTRACTS. TRANSACTIONS ON MARKETS LOCATED OUTSIDE THE UNITED STATES, INCLUDING MARKETS FORMALLY LINKED TO A UNITED STATES MARKET, MAY BE SUBJECT TO REGULATIONS WHICH OFFER DIFFERENT OR DIMIN-

ISHED PROTECTION TO THE POOL AND ITS PARTICIPANTS. FURTHER, UNITED STATES REGULATORY AUTHORITIES MAY BE UNABLE TO COMPEL THE ENFORCEMENT OF THE RULES OF REGULATORY AUTHORITIES OR MARKETS IN NON-UNITED STATES JURISDICTIONS WHERE TRANSACTIONS FOR THE POOL MAY BE EFFECTED.

If the potential liability of a participant in the pool is greater than the amount of the participant's contribution for the purchase of an interest in the pool and the profits earned thereon, whether distributed or not, the CPO must prominently disclose the following in the last paragraph of the Risk Disclosure Statement:

ALSO, BEFORE YOU DECIDE TO PARTICIPATE IN THIS POOL, YOU SHOULD NOTE THAT YOUR POTENTIAL LIABILITY AS A PARTICIPANT IN THIS POOL FOR TRADING LOSSES AND OTHER EXPENSES OF THE POOL IS NOT LIMITED TO THE AMOUNT OF YOUR CONTRIBUTION FOR THE PURCHASE OF AN INTEREST IN THE POOL AND ANY PROFITS EARNED THEREON. A COMPLETE DESCRIPTION OF THE LIABILITY OF A PARTICIPANT IN THIS POOL IS EXPLAINED MORE FULLY IN THIS DISCLOSURE DOCUMENT.

If the pool may engage in retail forex transactions, the Risk Disclosure Statement must further state:

YOU SHOULD ALSO BE AWARE THAT THIS COMMODITY POOL MAY ENGAGE IN OFF-EXCHANGE FOREIGN CURRENCY TRADING. SUCH TRADING IS NOT CONDUCTED IN THE INTERBANK MARKET. THE FUNDS THAT THE POOL USES FOR OFF-EXCHANGE FOREIGN CURRENCY TRADING WILL NOT RECEIVE THE SAME PROTECTIONS AS FUNDS USED TO MARGIN OR GUARANTEE EXCHANGE-TRADED FUTURES AND OPTION CONTRACTS. IF THE POOL DEPOSITS SUCH FUNDS WITH A COUNTERPARTY AND THAT COUNTERPARTY BECOMES INSOLVENT, THE POOL'S CLAIM FOR AMOUNTS DEPOSITED OR PROFITS EARNED ON TRANSACTIONS WITH THE COUNTERPARTY MAY NOT BE TREATED AS A COMMODITY CUSTOMER CLAIM FOR PURPOSES OF SUBCHAPTER IV OF CHAPTER 7 OF THE BANKRUPTCY CODE AND THE REGULATIONS THEREUNDER. THE POOL MAY BE A GENERAL

CREDITOR AND ITS CLAIM MAY BE PAID, ALONG WITH THE CLAIMS OF OTHER GENERAL CREDITORS, FROM ANY MONIES STILL AVAILABLE AFTER PRIORITY CLAIMS ARE PAID. EVEN POOL FUNDS THAT THE COUNTERPARTY KEEPS SEPARATE FROM ITS OWN FUNDS MAY NOT BE SAFE FROM THE CLAIMS OF PRIORITY AND OTHER GENERAL CREDITORS.

Table of Contents

The Document must contain a table of contents showing, by subject matter, the location of the disclosures made in the Disclosure Document. The table of contents must appear immediately following the Risk Disclosure Statement.

ADDITIONAL DISCLOSURES BY CTAs AND CPOs

CTAs and CPOs are required to disclose performance data as well as the details relating to the experience and background of the firm's principals. Both CTAs and CPOs are required to disclose the business history for the firm and the firm's principals for the preceding 5 years. Additionally, any regulatory action taken against the firm or its principals in the preceding 5 years must also be disclosed to prospective investors. Performance data for the CTAs as well as its principals must be disclosed for 5 years as well as for the current year. The entire performance history of the adviser must be disclosed if the CTA has less than 5 years of data available. If the adviser is just starting out and has not previously directed or advised accounts that fact must be disclosed to prospects. CTAs must disclose the method under which it will charge fees to clients in addition to the amount and timing of when the fees will be deducted. All disclosure documents must be made available for inspection by the CFTC with 72 hours' notice. In addition to the above CPOs must disclose the following:

- Principal office for the CPO
- Principal office for each commodity pool
- Types of contracts and options traded
- Restrictions on liquidation or liquidation procedures
- Name of all CTAs who manage 10% or more of a pool
- Name of any participant who owns 10% or more of a pool
- Name of executing FCM
- Minimum or maximum size of each pool
- Breakeven analysis for each pool showing what the fund must return for the investor to brekeven net of all fees

Established CPOs must make performance disclosures for the current year and for the preceding 5 years. If the pool has been in existence for between 3 and 5 years the entire history must be disclosed. If the pool has operated for less than 3 years the CPO must disclose the performance of all other pools for the last 3 years in addition to the complete performance history of the pool in question. If the CPO is a new CPO and has not previously operated a pool this exact language must be provided to investors "this pool has not commenced and does not have any performance history." All disclosure documents for CTAs and CPOs must be given to clients 48 hours prior to investing or at the time the account is opened if clients are given 5 days to terminate.

CUSTOMER ACCOUNTS

Prior to executing a customer's order, the firm must open an account for the customer. NFA Rule 2-30 "know your customer" states that an associated person should obtain all vital information relating to the customer. Series 3 candidates will see a number of questions dealing with customer accounts on their exam. Prior to opening an account for any new customer, an associated person must complete and sign a commodities account form and the account must be accepted by a manager or principal of the firm. The manager will acknowledge the acceptance of the account by signing the new account card. The associated person is responsible for ensuring that all customers are given the commodities risk disclosure statement to be signed and dated by all parties to the account at or before the time the account is opened and before any trades may be executed. By signing the risk disclosure document, the customer acknowledges that they have read the risk document and that they understand the risks of trading commodities futures contracts and options on commodity futures contracts. A copy of the signed risk disclosure statement must be kept by the introducing broker as well as by the futures commission merchant. The required risk disclosure for trading options on futures contracts may be disclosed in a separate document or in a combined risk disclosure document detailing the risks of trading futures and the risks of trading options on futures. The risk disclosure for options must contain a detailed explanation regarding the intrinsic value and time value of an option's premium. Account ownership is divided into five main types:

1. Individual
2. Joint
3. Corporate

4. Trust

5. Partnership

The associated person should try to obtain as much information about the customer as possible. The representative should obtain:

- Full name and address.
- Home and work phone numbers.
- Social security or tax ID number.
- Employer, occupation, and employer's address.
- Net worth.
- Investment and futures trading experience.
- Estimated annual income.
- Bank/brokerage firm reference.
- Whether they are employed by a bank or broker dealer.
- Any third-party trading authority.
- Citizenship.
- Legal age.
- How account was obtained.
- Whether client is officer, director, or 10% stockholder of a publicly traded company.

Customers who do not wish to disclose financial information may still open an account, if there is reason to believe that the customer can afford to maintain the account. All associated persons should update the customer's information regularly and note any changes in the following:

- Address
- Phone number
- Employer
- Investment objectives
- Marital status

Once the information has been provided by the customer, the associated person is not required to verify the information with third parties. The customer is the sole source of information relating to their financial profile.

INDIVIDUAL ACCOUNT

An individual account is an account that is owned by one person. That person makes the determination as to what futures contracts or options are purchased and sold. In addition, that person receives all of the distributions from the account.

JOINT ACCOUNT

A joint account is an account that is owned by two or more adults. Each party to the account may enter orders and request distributions. The associated person handling the account does not need to confirm instructions with both parties. Joint accounts require the owners to sign a joint account agreement prior to the opening of the account and the commodities risk disclosure document. Checks drawn from the account must be made out in the names of all of the parties. An associated person may maintain a joint account with another customer as long as it is approved by the firm. The exchange must be notified of the existence of the joint account and the associated person's percentage ownership and participation in the account. Confirmations must be sent to the customer with whom the associated person maintains the account. An introducing broker must give written permission to an FCM to carry the account of an associated person and the IB must receive duplicate confirmations and statements for the associated person's account.

JOINT TENANTS WITH RIGHTS OF SURVIVORSHIP

In a joint account with rights of survivorship (JTWROS), all the assets are transferred into the name of the surviving party in the event of one tenant's death. The surviving party becomes the sole owner of all of the assets in the account. Both parties on the account have an equal and undivided interest in the assets in the account.

JOINT TENANTS IN COMMON

In a joint tenants in common (JTIC) account, if one party dies all the assets of the tenant who has died become the property of the decedent's estate. They do not become the property of the surviving tenant. An account registered as joint tenants in common allows the assets in the account to be divided unequally. One party on the account could own 60% of the account's assets.

TRANSFER ON DEATH

An account that has been registered as a transfer on death (TOD) account allows the account owner to stipulate to whom the account is to go in the event of their death. The party who will become the owner of the account in the event of the account holder's death is known as the beneficiary. The beneficiary may only enter orders for the account if they have power of attorney for the account. Unlike an account that is registered as JTWROS, the assets in the account will not be at risk should the beneficiary be the subject of a lawsuit, such as in a divorce proceeding.

DEATH OF A CUSTOMER

If an agent is notified of the death of a customer, the agent must immediately cancel all open orders, liquidate any open futures or options positions, and mark the account deceased. The agent must await instructions from the executor or administrator of the estate. The death of a customer with a discretionary account automatically terminates the discretionary authority.

PARTNERSHIP ACCOUNTS

When a professional organization, such as a law partnership, opens an account, the associated person must obtain a copy of the partnership agreement. The partnership agreement will state who may enter orders for the account of the partnership. The purchase of futures contracts must not be prohibited by the partnership agreement.

CORPORATE ACCOUNTS

Corporations, like individuals, will purchase and sell futures contracts. In order to open a corporate account, the associated person must obtain a corporate resolution that states which individuals have the power to enter orders for the corporation. The associated person must obtain a corporate charter and the by-laws that state that the corporation may trade futures. Finally, a certificate of incumbency must be obtained for the officers who are authorized to transact business for the corporation within 60 days of the account opening.

DISCRETIONARY TRADING AUTHORIZATION

From time to time, people other than the beneficial owner of the account may be authorized to enter orders for the account. All discretionary authority must be evidenced in writing. A discretionary account allows the associated person to determine the following, without consulting the client first:

- The asset to be purchased or sold
- The amount of contracts to be purchased or sold
- The action to be taken in the account, whether to buy or sell

The principal of the firm must accept the account and review it more frequently to ensure against abuses. The principal must approve all discretionary trades within 1 business day of execution. The customer is required to sign a limited power of attorney that awards discretion to the associated person. The customer is bound by the decisions of the associated person, but may still enter orders for themselves. Once discretion is given to the associated person, they may not in turn give discretion to another party. If the associated person leaves the firm or stops managing the customer's account, the discretionary authority is automatically terminated. A full power of attorney allows an individual to deposit and withdraw cash and securities from the account. A full power of attorney is usually not given to an associated person. A full power of attorney is more appropriate for fiduciaries such as a trustee.

MANAGING DISCRETIONARY ACCOUNTS

All discretionary accounts must have the proper paperwork kept in the account file and must have:

- Every order entered marked discretionary, if discretion was exercised by the associated person.
- Every order approved promptly by a principal no later than the day after the trade date.
- A designated principal to review the account.
- A record of all transactions.
- An associated person must have a minimum of 2 years' experience to exercise discretion over a customer's account.

Discretionary authority will not be deemed to have been exercised if the customer provides the following:

- The action to buy or sell futures
- The specific commodity

- The specific delivery month and year
- The number of contracts

The associated person may determine the best time and price without having written power of attorney for the account.

ARBITRATION

The NFA's arbitration procedure provides parties with a forum to resolve disputes. Most claims submitted to arbitration are financial in nature, although other claims may be submitted. Arbitration provides a cost-effective alternative to dispute resolution and many disputes will be resolved much sooner than they otherwise may have been in court. All industry members are required to settle all disputes through arbitration. A public customer, however, must agree in writing to settle any dispute through arbitration. When a customer opens an account with a commodities firm, the firm will often have the customer sign a customer agreement, although not required by industry standards. The customer agreement usually contains a pre-dispute arbitration clause where the customer agrees to settle any dispute that may arise in arbitration rather than in court.

THE ARBITRATION PROCESS

Arbitration begins when an aggrieved party, known as the claimant, files a statement of claim, along with a submission agreement with the NFA. The party bringing the claim has 2 years from the date of discovery to take action. The party alleged to have caused the claimant harm must respond to the statement of claim promptly and is known as the respondent. If the amount involved in the claim is over $50,000, the respondent must answer the claim within 45 days. If the amount is less than $50,000, the respondent must answer the claim in 20 days. Dispute resolution through arbitration is available for matters involving:

- Member vs. member.
- Bank vs. member.
- Member vs. bank.
- Member vs. associated person.

- Associated person vs. member.
- Customer vs. member.
- Member vs. customer.

For disputes involving amounts in dispute of $50,000 or less, one arbitrator reviews the case and renders a decision. Larger disputes involving claims between $50,000 and $100,000 will be submitted to a panel of up to three arbitrators to render a decision on the matter. A hearing will take place and evidence and testimony will be presented to the panel. The number of arbitrators must always be odd. For disputes exceeding $100,000, three arbitrators will be assigned to hear the case.

THE CFTC REPARATION PROCESS

If a customer is claiming a violation of the Commodities Exchange Act or CFTC rule, the customer may take action against the firm or associated person by initiating proceedings with the CFTC. The proceedings will be heard by an administrative law judge and decided according to the type of procedure initiated. There are three procedures, as follows:

1. **Voluntary Decisional Procedure**—Requires the agreement of both parties. A judgment officer will render an expedited decision that is final and binding and cannot be appealed.

2. **Summary Decisional Procedure**—If the amount in question does not exceed $10,000, a decision may be made with or without a hearing. A hearing will be held only if requested. Parties agree to have a decision rendered through the submission of papers.

3. **Formal Decisional Procedure**—If the amount in question exceeds $10,000, either party may elect to resolve the dispute through a formal hearing.

AWARDS UNDER ARBITRATION

Parties to the proceedings will be notified of the decisions within 30 days. Awards under arbitration are final and binding; there is no appeal. If a monetary payment has been awarded, the party required to pay has 30 days to comply with the decision. A member or associated person who fails to pay an award under arbitration is subject to suspension.

CURRENCY TRANSACTIONS

All member firms must guard against money laundering. Every member must report any currency receipt of $10,000 or more from any one customer on a single day. The firm must fill out and submit a currency transaction report, also known as Form 4789, to the Internal Revenue Service (IRS) within 15 days of the receipt of the currency. Multiple deposits that total $10,000 or more will also require the firm to file a currency transaction report (CTR). Additionally, the firm is required to maintain a record of all international wire transfers of $3,000 or greater.

THE PATRIOT ACT

The Patriot Act, as part of the Bank Secrecy Act, requires firms to have written policies and procedures designed to detect suspicious activity. The firm must designate a principal to ensure compliance with the firm's policies and to train firm personnel. The firm is required to file a Suspicious Activity Report for any transaction of more than $5,000 that appears questionable. Anti-money-laundering rules require that all firms implement a customer identification program to ensure that the firm knows the true identity of their customers. All customers who open an account with the firm, as well as individuals with trading authority, are subject to this rule. The firm must ensure that its customers do not appear on any list of known or suspected terrorists. A firm's anti-money-laundering program must be approved by senior management.

The money laundering process begins with the placement of the funds. This is when the money is deposited in an account with the firm. The second step of the laundering process is known as layering. The layering process will consist of multiple deposits in amounts less than $10,000. The funds will often be drawn from different financial institutions; this is also known as structuring. The launderers will then purchase and sell futures or securities in the account. The integration of the proceeds back into the banking system completes the process. At this point, the launderers may use the money to purchase goods and services if they appear to have come from legitimate sources. Firms must also identify the customers who open the account and must make sure that they are not conducting business with anyone on the OFAC list. This list is maintained by the Treasury Department Office of Foreign Assets Control (OFAC). It consists of known and suspected terrorists, criminals, and members of pariah nations. Conducting business with anyone on this list is strictly prohibited. Associated persons who aid the laundering of money are subject to prosecution and face up to 20 years in prison and a $500,000 fine per transaction. The associated person does not have to be involved in the scheme or even know about it to be prosecuted.

U.S. ACCOUNTS

Every member must obtain from U.S. customers:

- A social security number/documentation number
- Date of birth
- Address
- Place of business

FOREIGN ACCOUNTS

All non-U.S. customers must provide at least one of the following:

- A Passport number and country of issuance
- An alien ID number
- A U.S. tax ID number
- A number from another form of government-issued ID and the name of the issuing country

IDENTITY THEFT

The fraudulent practice of identity theft may be used by criminals in an attempt to obtain access to the assets or credit of another person. The Federal Trade Commission (FTC) requires banks and broker dealers to establish and maintain written identity theft prevention programs. A broker dealer's written supervisory procedures manual must reference its identity theft program. The program must be designed to detect red flags relating to the known suspicious activity employed during an attempt at identity theft. The identity theft prevention program should be designed to allow the firm to respond quickly to any attempted identity theft to mitigate any potential damage.

ANNUAL COMPLIANCE QUESTIONNAIRE

On an annual basis, the NFA will send each NFA member FCM, RFED, IB, CPO, CTA, and LTM a business profile questionnaire relating to the member's business activities. The member must complete the questionnaire and submit the completed questionnaire on the date specified thereon. The NFA shall deem the failure to file the completed questionnaire within 30 days following such date a request to withdraw from NFA membership, and shall notify the member accordingly.

ETHICS TRAINING

NFA compliance Rule 2-9 requires that every NFA member establish and administer an ethics training program for its employees as part of the member's ongoing supervisory responsibility. The training program must comply with the guidelines laid out in the CTFC statement of acceptable practices. The program should include:

- An explanation of the rules and regulations to be covered
- Ethical obligations owed to the public
- How to assess customer suitability
- How to make proper disclosures to customers
- How to handle conflicts of interest
- How the program will be administered
- Who will administer the program

The member is allowed to determine the timing with regard to how and when the program is administered and is required to maintain records for attendance and completion of the program by its employees.

VIOLATIONS AND COMPLAINTS

The NFA's compliance rules set forth guidelines for the investigation of alleged violations and complaints against a member firm or associated person. The NFA staff originates many complaints against member firms and associated persons during their routine examinations of member firms. The NFA will conduct periodic unannounced onsite reviews of the member. Additionally, every member is subject to a full audit by the NFA every 24 months. Complaints and allegations of wrongdoing may also originate from a customer of the member firm or from another member. If an NFA staff member has received the complaint that alleges a violation of NFA regulations, it is up to the NFA to determine if the complaint has merit. The president of the NFA with the agreement of the board of directors may initiate a *member responsibility action*. The member responsibility action at its most severe could require the member who is in violation of NFA regulations to immediately cease business. This action may be taken with or without a hearing. In most cases, when the regional committee issues a complaint against a member or associated person, there are no restrictions placed upon the respondent during the time the complaint is being heard. Possible penalties, after having been found to have violated one or more of the association's rules, are:

- Censure or reprimand
- Suspension from association with a member for a specified time
- Expelled from membership for a period of time (2/3 vote required to impose)
- Fined $250,000 per violation
- Any other penalty deemed appropriate, such as restitution

The NFA's Regional Business Conduct Committee will have original jurisdiction over disciplinary proceedings for member firms within its region. The proceedings may be initiated at the request of the CFTC or the NFA's Department of Compliance. The respondent has the right to be represented by an attorney and the decision of the Regional Business Conduct Committee may be appealed to the Appeals Committee within 15 days of the decision. If the respondent wished to further appeal the decision of the Appeals Committee they may appeal the decision to the CFTC within 30 days. A final appeal may be made to the U.S. court system and the U.S. court of appeals.

POSITION REPORTING AND SPECULATIVE POSITION LIMITS

In order to prevent large investors from manipulating the price of a commodities future or the value of the underlying cash commodity, the exchanges have set both reporting and maximum limits for the size of a position established on the same side of the market. Both individuals and the member firms carrying the account are required to report certain large positions to the CFTC that are established for any account, or for any group of accounts acting in concert. Firms and investors must file a large position report once the position established exceeds the filing threshold on the same side of the market. For most contracts the current filing threshold is 200 contracts on the same side of the market. Firms and investors are required to file the initial LPR data, as well as any changes in reportable positions to the CFTC via a submission report. Reports are only required to be updated when there is:

- An increase in a reported position.
- A decrease in a reported position.
- A reported position is closed.

If a firm reports a large position for an account it is required to report any changes to that position as long as the position remains above the threshold limit. When calculating its position a firm must calculate its aggregate long or short positions on all exchanges for all delivery months to determine if the firm is in compliance with the speculative position limit. If the previously reported position falls below the contract threshold, the report only needs to be filed on the day the number of contracts falls below the reporting level. No subsequent reports are required for the position as long as the position remains below the threshold limit. The speculative position limit is the maximum number of contracts that may be held either long or short by an account or by a group of accounts acting in concert. The speculative position limit varies from contract to contract and the limit is greater than the number of contracts in the reporting threshold. Bonafide hedgers may be entitled to an exemption from these limits if they can demonstrate a business need for the exemption. It is important to note that anticipatory hedges are specifically included in the classification of a bona fide hedge. An anticipatory hedge is one established to off set a potential risk based on assumed future demand or production.

An investor who regularly engages in spread transactions does not meet the definition of a bona fide hedger.

WRITTEN COMMUNICATION WITH THE PUBLIC

Communication is defined as any written communication distributed or made available to public investors. The communication may be distributed in hard copy or in electronic formats. Public communications contain all components of advertising and promotional material and are governed by the standards of NFA Rule 2-29. All communications must adhere to fair and equitable trade practices and may not contain any false or misleading statements. Any opinions contained in the communication must be clearly indicated as opinions and not stated as facts. All communications must be approved by a principal prior to first use. Promotional material prepared by branch offices of guaranteed introducing brokers must be approved by the main office. NFA regulations prohibit members from using communications containing hypothetical calculations unless the member provides a special disclosure regarding the hypothetical calculation. If the member cites the rankings it has received from an outside business service for its managed accounts, the member must disclose the limitations of the ranking service. Any ranking system that does not adhere to CFTC guidelines must be clearly explained. If the member uses material that has been prepared by an outside firm the member is still responsible for insuring the content adheres to all NFA and CFTC regulations. All written communication must be maintained by the member for 5 years from the date of last use. The member must keep a separate onsite advertising file containing all promotional material and the approval of the material readily accessible for 3 years and for 5 years from the date the material was last used. All promotional material should follow NFA guidelines but are generally not required to be filled with the NFA.

 TAKE**NOTE!**

NFA regulations state that promotional items must contain risk disclosures that are "equally conspicuous" in terms of the impact the disclosures have in the material. The font and the number of times the word reward and risk appear in the materials or are said during seminars must all be equally balanced.

Particular issues can arise when trying to achieve a balance in the presentation of information verbally. Presentations made over the phone or during seminars should try to balance the amount of time dedicated to explaining the opportunities and risks of investing in futures. Should an AP discuss the opportunities of investing in futures with a potential client for 30 minutes during a phone call, the AP must spend a reasonable amount of time discussing the potential risks. If the AP does not spend a reasonable amount time going over the risks of investing in futures and merely offers to email or send the risk disclosures this would not be considered reasonable and balanced. This same standard is in place for live seminars. Streaming or other videos used to promote futures business must also balance the amount of time spent detailing the risks involved in futures investing. Most video promotions will add a canned risk disclosure at the end of the presentation but this alone may not be enough to meet NFA standards. Infomercials and appearances where the member pays for the time on TV or radio must make specific disclosures at the opening and closing of the presentation to make sure the audience knows that this is a paid promotion made by the member. Legitimate interviews that are under the control or direction of the TV, radio station or website are still deemed to be promotional activities and must try to balance the risks of futures during the interview. However, these interviews do not require the same opening and closing disclosures of an infomercial. Special care must be used when discussing the risks of trading options on futures. It is considered to be misleading if the speaker or promotional material simply states that trading options on futures has limited risk. Only certain long option positions have limited risk equal to the amount of the premium paid. Any mention of limited risk in option trading must clearly state this fact.

CUSTOMER CONFIRMATIONS

All customers must be sent a confirmation for each order executed in futures contracts in the customer's account. Industry rules require a confirmation of the transaction be sent to the customer no later than the business day following the transaction. The confirmation will contain the name of the FCM and the name of the IB if applicable. All customer confirmations must include:

- Customer's name and account number
- Account executive number
- Description of the transaction, that is buy or sell
- Trade date and settlement date
- Number of contracts
- Contract delivery month
- Price
- Amount due or owed
- Option specifics (open, closing, covered, uncovered)

CUSTOMER ACCOUNT STATEMENTS

All customers must receive account statements at least quarterly when there has been no activity in the account. A customer must receive a statement every month that there is activity in the account or when there is an open contract position. The account statement will contain the name of the FCM and the name of the IB if applicable. Examples of activity include:

- Purchases and sales
- Dividend and interest received
- Addition or withdrawal of cash or securities

  Customer account statements must show:

- All positions in the account.
- All activity since the last statement.
- All credit and debit balances.

A customer who wishes to transfer his/her account to another merchant will submit account transfer instructions. The firm that will be receiving the account will submit the transfer instructions to the customer's current merchant. The firm carrying the customer's account has 2 business days to validate the instructions and an additional 3 business days to complete the transfer. The transfer of a customer's open futures contract position from one FCM to another requires that an ex pit transaction take place between the carrying firm and the receiving firm. The clearinghouse recognizes the FCM as having the open futures contract position, not the customer. As such the FCMs must engage in an ex pit transaction. This transaction will close the open futures contract position at the carrying firm and open a futures contract position at the receiving firm. This transaction will be executed without any impact to the customer.

RECORD KEEPING

Futures commission merchants are required to maintain all customer confirmations and statements for each account carried by the FCM. The requirement to maintain these records applies to customers doing business directly with the FCM as well as those customers who have been introduced to the FCM by an introducing merchant or broker. The introducing broker is not required to maintain these records but may elect to do so. Both the IB and the FCM are required to maintain a daily journal of all orders received and placed. This journal should contain specifics about the order as well as the customer's name and account number. Both the IB and FCM are required to maintain customer account forms and signed risk disclosure statements. Most records are required to be kept for 2 years readily accessible and for 5 years total. CPOs must maintain a record of all transactions executed for each pool it operates, all statements received from an FCM, and records of all transactions executed for the account of its principals. CTAs must maintain the following at the main office:

- Names and address of each client
- Copies of all powers of attorney
- A list of all positions
- Copies of all statements and confirmations for all clients
- All communication with the public

All customer orders received by an AP must be properly handled and routed to the market for execution on a timely basis. To ensure that orders are properly routed and handled all FCMs must time stamp all crucial events during the life of an order. The events that are required to be documented and time stamped include:

- When the customer enters the order with his AP.
- When the order is routed to the market or called to the floor.
- When the order is executed.
- When the execution of the order is reported to the customer.
- When the order expired, was canceled or changed.

 TAKE**NOTE!**

An introducing broker who directs customer orders to its FCM must time stamp the order when its received by the customer. The FCM must also time stamp the order within 1 minute of receipt from the introducing broker.

BUSINESS CONTINUITY PLAN

NFA Rule 2-38 was one of the regulations developed as a result of the attack on 9/11. Rule 2-38 requires NFA member firms to develop and maintain plans and backup facilities to ensure that the firm can meet its obligations to its customers and counterparties in the event that its main facilities are damaged, destroyed, or are inaccessible. The plan must provide the firm with the ability to operate with minimal disruption to its business. The plan should also include the name and contact information for one or two firm representatives who may be contacted in the event of an emergency affecting the firm.

Pretest

1. The maximum amount one may be fined for each violation of the Commodity Exchange Act is:

   a. $10,000.

   b. $10,0000.

   c. $140,000.

   d. $1,400,000.

2. Which act requires that all transactions in commodities futures take place on the floor?

   a. The Grain Futures Act

   b. The Commodity Exchange Act

   c. The Commodities Trading Act

   d. The Commodity Floor Act

3. The ultimate regulator for the futures industry is:

   a. The CFTC.

   b. The NFA.

   c. Congress.

   d. The Federal Court System.

4. Any individual or organization that intends to transact futures business with members of the investing public must become registered with the National Futures Association (NFA).

   True

   False

5. Which of the following must register with the NFA?
   I. Futures Commission Merchant (FCM)
   II. Introducing Broker (IB)
   III. Commodity Pool Operator (CPO)
   IV. Commodity Trading Adviser (CTA)
      a. I and IV
      b. II and III
      c. I, II, and III
      d. I, II, III, and IV

6. Which of the following is allowed to hold customer funds?
   a. CPO
   b. CTA
   c. AP
   d. FCM

7. Registration as a CPO is required for CPOs who:
   a. Manage more than $1,000,000.
   b. Manage more than $10,000,000.
   c. Manage more than $400,000.
   d. Manage more than $500,000.

8. A CTA is someone who advises as to the value of futures contracts, options on futures, retail off-exchange forex contracts, or swaps.
   True
   False

9. Which of the following NFA registrants must always be an individual?
   a. AP
   b. FCM
   c. CTA
   d. CPO

10. An FCM that clears all of its transactions on an omnibus basis with a clearing member will have customer confirmations and statements produced by the clearing member.

    True

    False

11. All NFA members must complete the annual business profile questionnaire and submit the completed questionnaire:

    a. Within 10 business days.

    b. Within 30 days of year end.

    c. Within 15 business days.

    d. Within 30 days of the date stated by the NFA.

Answer Keys

CHAPTER 1: FUTURES AND FORWARDS

1. (B) The minimum quality grade that may be delivered to settle the obligations of a futures contract is known as the basis grade.

2. (False) Futures trading on the floor of the exchange takes place in the futures pit for the specific contract. No trades for futures contracts may take place away from the pit or outside the ring.

3. (A) The exchange's floor committee sets the rules for trading futures on the floor of the exchange and will resolve trading disputes between members.

4. (False) Because the terms and conditions for each forward contract is negotiated on an individual basis, it is extremely difficult to find another party to take over the obligation under the contract should circumstances change between the contract date and the delivery date. There is no secondary market for forward contracts.

5. (D) The transactions between the producer or seller of the commodity and the user or buyer of the commodity take place in the spot or cash market.

6. (True) The counterparty risk has been eliminated through performance guarantees. So even if one party defaults, the clearinghouse will make sure the other party is made whole.

7. (D) The delivery of the underlying commodity is delivered to an exchange-approved warehouse.

8. (B) All of the items listed must be included in the notice of delivery except there is no margin release form.

9. (False) Certain exchanges require that the buyer accept delivery of the commodity and do not allow the buyer to offset the delivery requirement by selling the same futures contract. This is known as a stopped delivery notice.

10. (D) A seller who wishes to deliver the commodity may notify his broker of the intention to deliver the commodity on the first notice day.

CHAPTER 2: TRADING COMMODITY FUTURES

1. (C) A buy stop order is placed above the market and is used to protect against a loss or to protect a profit on a short sale of futures contracts.

2. (B) A market on open order will be executed during the opening time range. The exchange sets an opening time range that is considered to be the open of the trading day. All orders executed during this time will be considered to have been executed on the open. If the order is not executed during this time, it is canceled.

3. (A) The only order that will not get executed or expire within seconds of it being presented to the market is the all-or-none order. An all-or-none order can be a day order or may be entered GTC.

4. (True) With this type of order the investor wants the order to be executed if the market trades at or through a set price. Unlike a limit order, the MIT order becomes a market order to purchase or sell the contracts at the next available price.

5. (C) A CFO or cancels former order is entered when an investor wishes to change the terms of an existing order. An investor may be making a change to a limit price, may be making a change to the number of contracts, or may be changing the order from a day order to a GTC order.

6. (C) A basis order may be entered by an investor to execute the order if the spread between 2 contract months for the same commodity reaches a certain range or based on the relationship between the price of two related commodities.

7. (C) A client who wishes to remain anonymous may ask their futures commission merchant (FCM) to give the order out to another FCM for execution to protect their identity.

8. (B) A scale order is entered when an investor wishes to establish or offset a position by purchasing or selling futures contracts at specified intervals.

9. (True) With a not held (NH) or disregard the tape (DRT) order, the investor gives discretion to the floor broker as to the time and price of execution.

CHAPTER 3: FUTURES PRICING

1. (C) A corn contract represents 5,000 bushels of corn and is priced in centers per bushel.

2. (False) The minimum price variation is known as a tick, however the tick size is set by the exchange, not the CFTC.

3. (C) The daily price limits for a given commodity contract are established by the board of directors at the exchange where the futures contract trades. All daily price limits set by the exchange are subject to review and approval of the Commodity Futures Trading Commission (CFTC).

4. (False) The Chicago Mercantile Exchange (CME) does not automatically increase the margin requirement when the daily price limit expands.

5. (D) The amount of par value covered under a treasury bond futures contract is 1 bond with $100,000 par value.

6. (C) A crop year for a commodity covers the time when the commodity is harvested by farmers and runs until the harvest period of the following year.

7. (D) A T-bill contract covers a 3-month T-bill with $1,000,000 par value. To determine the value of the tick, multiply 1 basis point times $1,000,000 and divide by 4, as follows: .0001 × $1,000,000 = $100 $100 ÷ 4 = $25.

8. (False) The S&P 500 contract settles in cash and not with the delivery of shares of the 500 companies.

9. (D) An investor would buy foreign currency futures for all of the following reasons except if the government in that country is replaced by a new regime. Political instability is never good for a country.

10. (A) The investor has made 25 points or $6,250 on the contract. The profit per contract is found by multiplying the 25-point profit by the value of each point. Each S&P point is worth $250. In this case 25 × $250 = $6,250.

CHAPTER 4: PRICE FORECASTING

1. (C) A market that has distant contract months trading at prices higher than near-term contract months is said to be contango, a premium market, a carrying charge market, or a normal market.

2. (True) As the delivery month approaches, the price of the cash commodity and spot futures contract will converge, effectively pricing the contract during the delivery period as if it was equal to the cash commodity.

3. (C) The premium in prices for each successive delivery month is based in part on the carrying charge for the commodity.

4. (A) The carrying charges for the cash commodity are storage fees, insurance, and any interest the owner may have to pay if he is carrying the commodity using borrowed funds. There is no margin interest associated with a cash commodity or with a commodity futures contract.

5. (False) The company in this case should purchase wheat futures for delivery in 3 months as it would be cheaper. The total carrying costs for wheat is 4 cents plus 1.5 cents or 5.5 cents per month × 3 months equals 16.5 cents in total carrying charges. Total cost to purchase and carry wheat for 3 months is 5.665 cents per bushel. The company can purchase wheat futures for delivery 3 months from now for 5.65 and save 1.5 cents per bushel.

6. (D) During times of supply shortages the market for a given commodity may become inverted, where the price of the cash commodity is trading at a premium to the futures contract prices.

7. (B) For the grain complex both the CFTC and CBOT report the supply of grains available for delivery. These reports are published weekly.

8. (False) Resistance is created at the point to which the commodity appreciates and attracts sellers. The new sellers that are brought into the market, because of the higher price, create supply for the commodity and prevent it from rising any further.

9. (B) The higher the open interest is in a contract, the higher the liquidity will be in that contract. This is because there are more parties interested in trading the contract.

10. (B) New buyers and sellers are entering the market establishing new positions and the buyers are more aggressive driving prices higher. This is a technically strong market.

CHAPTER 5: SPECULATION AND HEDGING

1. (False) The motive of a speculator is to realize a profit on a position in a futures contract based on change in the value of the futures contract. A hedger is trying to reduce risk, not earn a profit on futures trading.

2. (A) The trader made $1.75 per barrel or $1,750 per contract ($1.75 × 1,000 barrels). The trader bought and sold 3 contracts of crude oil and realized a profit of $5,250 (3 × $1,750).

3. (D) To determine the profit or loss on a trade in a gold futures contract, the profit or loss must be multiplied by 100 troy ounces per contract.

4. (C) Initial margin is the amount of money that must be deposited to establish a futures position. The amount is set by the board of directors of the exchange on which the contract trades and the amount is the same for both long and short contract positions.

5. (A) The trader was short the contract and the price of the gold contract increased from 1425 to 1431, moving against the trader and causing the margin equity in the trader's account to fall. The trader deposited $75 per ounce or $7,500 total ($75 × 100 ounces). The price of the contract moved against the trader by $6 per ounce or $600 for the contract. As a result the trader's equity fell from $7,500 to $6,900.

6. (D) The open trade equity is calculated based on the initial margin deposit plus or minus any unrealized profit or loss on the open contract position.

7. (False) Hedgers take futures positions that are opposite to their position in the underlying cash commodity.

8. (D) The storage operator's effective selling price was 5.16 per bushel. The operator sold the wheat in the cash market at 5.11 and made 5 cents on the short July futures contract. 5.11 per bushel plus 5 cents per bushel profit on the futures gives the operator an effective selling price of 5.16 per bushel.

9. (False) If cash corn its trading at 4.70 per bushel and the near-term futures contract is trading at 4.82 per bushel, corn is trading at 12 cents under.

10. (C) If the price of the cash commodity falls and the price of the futures rises, a person who needs to purchase the cash commodity will have the best possible outcome. The cash price of the commodity has fallen and they will have made a profit on their long futures, reducing their effective purchase price.

CHAPTER 6: COMMODITY FUTURES OPTIONS AND COMMODITY FUTURES SPREADS

1. (A) The investor will break even if silver is trading at 19.25 at expiration. To determine the breakeven, add the premium of the call to the strike price. In this case, 18 + 1.25 = 19.25.

2. (False) When an investor sells a put their maximum loss is not unlimited because the price of the futures contract cannot fall below zero. The maximum loss for a put seller equals the strike price of the put minus the amount of premium they received when they sold the put.

3. (B) The time value of an option is the amount by which the premium exceeds the intrinsic or in the money amount. The calls on the July wheat futures contract are 14 cents in the money. Therefore the time value in the July 5 calls is 3 cents.

4. (D) Options on Treasury futures are also quoted as a percentage of par down, but are priced in increments of 64ths of 1%.

5. (True) A long straddle is the simultaneous purchase of a call and a put on the same futures contract with the same strike price and expiration month. An option investor would purchase a straddle when they expect the futures contract price to be extremely volatile and to make a significant move in either direction.

6. (B) Because the investor has sold both options in a short straddle, the investor's maximum gain is equal to the premiums received.

7. (B) The investor who established this put spread is bearish and believes that the price of March wheat will fall. The spread is a debit put spread and is a vertical put spread.

8. (False) A diagonal spread consists of one long option and one short option of the same class that have different strike prices and expiration months.

9. (D) The investor paid 7 cents per pound as the premium for the feeder cattle call. Each feeder cattle contract covers 50,000 pounds, so the investor paid $3,500 per contract and purchased 2 contracts for a total premium of $7,000.

10. (C) The investor who is long gold would have to sell a futures contract on a related metal to establish a spread. Of the choices listed, only selling December platinum would create a product spread.

CHAPTER 7: CFTC & NFA AND REGULATIONS

1. (C) The maximum amount one may be fined for each violation of the Commodity Exchange Act is $140,000.

2. (B) The Commodity Exchange Act of 1936 replaced the Grain Futures Act of 1922 and required that any transaction in commodity futures or commodity futures options take place on the floor of an exchange and not in the over the counter or OTC market.

3. (A) The CFTC is a direct government agency and is the ultimate regulator in the commodity futures industry.

4. (True) Any individual or organization who intends to transact futures business with members of the investing public must become registered with the National Futures Association (NFA).

5. (D) All of the entities listed must register with the NFA in order to conduct commodities business with the public.

6. (D) A futures commission merchant may also hold customer funds as margin or to guarantee customer futures contracts. An FCM must have minimum net capital of at least $1,000,000.

7. (C) Registration as a CPO is required for CPOs who manage a pool or a group of pools with more than $400,000 in total assets in all pools.

8. (True) A commodity trading adviser or CTA is an individual or business who, for compensation or profit, advises others on trading futures contracts or options on futures contracts. A CTA is also someone who advises as to the value of futures contracts, options on futures, retail off-exchange forex contracts, or swaps.

9. (A) An AP is an individual who solicits orders, customers, or customer funds or who supervises persons engaged in these activities on behalf of an FCM, IB, CTA, or CPO.

10. (False) If the FCM clears its trades on an omnibus basis, all transactions are cleared through one account and the clearing member does not know for whom the trade was executed. The introducing member is required to send customer confirmations and statements if they clear through an omnibus account.

11. (D) The NFA shall deem the failure to file the completed questionnaire within 30 days following the stated date a request to withdraw from NFA membership, and shall notify the member accordingly.

Glossary of Exam Terms

A

Act
The Commodity Exchange Act of 1936 replaced the Grain Futures Act of 1922 and required that any transaction in commodity futures or commodity futures options take place on the floor of an exchange and not in the over the counter or OTC market.

actual funds
The equity in each commodity trading account over which a CTA has full discretionary authority and may enter trades and withdraw funds without the client's consent.

actuals
The underling physical cash commodity.

Appeals Committee
The Appeals Committee, established under NFA Bylaws, is to whom a respondent may contest the findings of the business conduct committee.

approved delivery facility
Is an exchange-approved warehouse or storage facility authorized to accept delivery of underlying commodities for the settlement of futures contracts.

arbitrage
An investment strategy used to profit from market inefficiencies between two contracts or between the price of the futures contract and the price of the underlying commodity.

arbitration
A forum provided by the NFA to resolve disputes between two parties. Only a public customer may not be forced to settle a dispute through arbitration. The public customer must agree to arbitration in writing. All industry participants must settle disputes through arbitration.

associated person
Any individual under the control of a futures commission merchant (FCM) or introducing broker (IB), including employees, officers, and directors, as well as those individuals who act in any sales capacity or who supervise such.

B

backwardation   A pricing structure where distant futures contracts are trading at progressively lower prices to near-term contracts. Also known as an inverted market.

basis   The term used to describe the price spread between the price of the underlying cash commodity and the futures contract.

basis grade   A minimum standard for the quality of a commodity that may be delivered under the settlement of a futures contract.

basis point   Measures a bond's yield; 1 basis point is equal to 1/100 of 1%.

bearish   An investor's belief that prices will decline.

bear market   A market condition that is characterized by continually falling prices and a series of lower lows in overall prices.

bid   A price that an investor or merchant is willing to pay for a futures contract. It is also a price at which an investor may sell a contract immediately and the price at which a market maker will buy a security.

board of trade   An exchange duly recognized by the CFTC and authorized to trade futures contracts.

board order   *See* market if touched order.

breakout   A technical term used to describe the price action of a security when it increases past resistance to a higher level and into a new trading range.

broker   An individual or firm that acts as the customer's agent and executes futures orders for a commission.

bullish   An investor who believes that the price of a security or prices as a whole will rise is said to be bullish.

bull market   A market condition that is characterized by rising prices and a series of higher highs.

Business Conduct Committee   The Business Conduct Committee, established under NFA Bylaws, issues complaints against members for rule violations.

C

call option   A type of option that gives the holder the right to purchase a specified number of futures contracts at a stated price for a specified period of time.

carrying firm   An FCM who clears customer trades and has custody of or carries customer assets.

carrying charge	The cost to store, insure, and finance the physical possession of the underlying commodity.
carrying charge market	A pricing structure where distant month contracts trade at a premium to near-term contracts, representing the cost to store, insure, and finance the physical possession of the underlying commodity.
carryover	The amount of a commodity that remains available from the previous harvest year.
cash commodity	The actual physical commodity. *See* actuals.
cash market	The market where the actual commodity is sold and delivered upon receipt of cash payment.
certified stock	The amount of the cash commodity on hand and in warehouses and approved for settlement of futures contracts. Also known as deliverable stock.
churning	Executing transactions that are excessive in their frequency or size in light of the resources of the account for the purpose of generating commissions.
clearing	The process by which the clearinghouse guarantees the performance of each futures contract for each buyer and seller.
clearinghouse	An agency that guarantees and settles futures and option transactions for an exchange.
clearing member	A member of both the exchange and of the clearinghouse who may carry customer funds and clear trades.
closing order	*See* closing range.
closing range	A range of prices at which trades occurred during the exchange-stipulated closing time frame.
closing transaction	An order to offset an existing long or short futures or option contract position.
commission or CFTC	The CFTC was created by Congress to oversee the trading in all futures contracts. The CFTC is a direct government agency and is the ultimate regulator in the commodity futures industry. The CFTC is not a self-regulatory organization (SRO).
commission house/ commission merchant	A firm that represents customer orders for the purchase and sale of commodity futures contracts and options on commodity futures contracts. The firm charges a fee known as a commission for executing the customers' orders
Commodity Exchange Act	The Commodity Exchange Act of 1936 replaced the Grain Futures Trading Act of 1922. It was amended in 1975 and the Commodity Futures Trading Commission or CFTC was created by Congress to oversee the trading in all futures contracts. The CFTC is a direct government agency and is the ultimate regulator in the commodity futures industry.

commodity futures contract	An exchange-approved contract representing the obligation to accept or make delivery of a set amount of the underlying commodity.
commodity futures option	A contract that creates the right to purchase or sell a futures contract in the case of the buyer of the option or the obligation to purchase or sell the futures contract in the case of the seller.
commodity pool	A business entity established to trade commodities in a single account established from the combined contributions of numerous participants.
commodity pool operator or CPO	A Commodity Pool Operator or CPO is an organization which invests money contributed by a group of participants to a single account for the purpose of investing the money in futures contracts, options on futures, retail off-exchange forex contracts or swaps, or to invest in another commodity pool.
commodity trading adviser or CTA	A commodity trading adviser or CTA is an individual or business who, for compensation or profit, advises others on trading futures contracts or options on futures contracts. A CTA is also someone who advises as to the value of futures contracts, options on futures, retail off-exchange forex contracts, or swaps.
congestion	A sideways trading pattern characterized by small price changes with support and resistance being in very close proximity to each other.
contango	A futures contract pricing structure where the further delivery months trade at successively higher premiums. This market structure is also known as a premium market, a normal market, or a carrying charge market.
contract	A standardized agreement to accept or to make delivery of a commodity in the case of a futures contract or of a futures contract in the case of a commodity futures option.
contract grades	The various grades of the commodity that may be delivered to settle a futures contract. The contract grades are basis grade (standard), premium, and discount grade.
contract market	An exchange officially designated by the CFTC where commodities futures and commodity futures options trading may take place.
contract month	The month during which the underlying commodity must be delivered by the seller and during which delivery must be accepted by the buyer.
contract unit	The standardized number of units of the underlying commodity covered by the futures contract.
controlled account	An account where discretionary authority to purchase and sell commodity futures contracts has been given to a third party.

corner	The accumulation or control of a substantial amount of the supply of the commodity, to the point where the parties controlling the substantial supply can dictate the price for the commodity or manipulate the price of the commodity in the marketplace.
cover	The act of offsetting a short futures position by purchasing the contract to close and exit the market.
covered call	The sale of a call option against a long futures contract position.
credit spread	An option position that results in a net premium or credit received by the investor from the simultaneous purchase and sale of 2 calls or 2 puts on the same futures contract.
crop year	The period for agricultural commodities which begins with the current harvest and runs until the next harvest of the following year.

D

daily price limit	The maximum amount by which the price of a given commodity may rise or fall during a given trading day.
day order	An order that will be canceled at the end of the trading day on which it is entered, if not executed.
day trader	An investor who seeks to profit from the intraday price changes of futures contracts and who does not hold these positions overnight.
debit spread	An option position that results in a net premium paid by the investor from the simultaneous purchase and sale of 2 calls or 2 puts on the same security.
deferred futures	Futures contracts with expiration dates exceeding the current or front month contract.
delivery	The presentation of the underlying commodity to settle the obligations of a futures contract.
delivery notice	A written notice submitted to a long futures contract holder informing them of their requirement to accept delivery of the physical commodity on a specified date from the short futures contract holder.
delta	A measure of an option's price change in relation to a price change in the underlying security.
depository receipt	A receipt issued as evidence of the ownership of the underlying cash commodity.
discount	A lower contract settlement price paid by the buyer to accept delivery of an inferior or discount grade commodity to settle a futures contract.

discount market	A futures contract pricing structure where the near-term contract is trading at a higher price than the more distant contracts. This is also known as an inverted market or backwardation.
discretionary account	*See* controlled account.

E

equity	The total cash value of an account, including margin deposits plus or minus any realized or unrealized profit and loss on futures contracts.
euro	The single European currency used by numerous countries as legal tender.
exercise price	The price at which an option investor may purchase or sell a futures contract.
expiration	The date on which an option ceases to exist and all rights and obligations are eliminated.
ex-pit transaction	A trade that is executed outside of the futures trading pit. An exchange for physical order would be an example of an ex-pit transaction where the actual commodity is exchanged for a futures contract position, not as settlement of the contract.

F

fill-or-kill order (FK)	A type of order that requires that all of the contracts in the order be purchased or sold immediately or not at all.
financial futures	Contracts based on Treasury securities, interest rates, and stock market indexes.
floor broker	An individual member of an exchange who may execute orders on the floor.
floor traders	Members of the exchange who trade for their own accounts. Also known as locals.
foreign board of trade	A futures exchange or market located outside of the United States, its territories, or possessions.
foreign currency futures	Contracts based on a specified number of units of another country's currency.
forwards	A two-party contract for the purchase and sale of a commodity delivered at a future date.
futures	A two-party contract. The specific terms and conditions of the contracts are standardized and set by the exchanges on which the futures contracts trade. The contract amount, delivery date, and type of settlement vary between the different types of futures contracts.

futures commission merchant or FCM	A person who is required to register or is registered as a futures commission merchant under the Act and Commission Rules.

G

Ginnie Mae	A government corporation that provides liquidity to the mortgage markets by purchasing pools of mortgages that have been insured by the Federal Housing Administration and the Veterans Administration. Ginnie Mae issues pass-through certificates to investors, backed by the pools of mortgages.
give-up order	A customer order that is given out by a merchant to be executed by another firm to protect the customer's identity.
gross processing margin	The calculation that determines the profit that can be made by processing the raw commodity into refined products.

H

head and shoulders	A chart pattern that indicates a reversal of a trend. A head-and-shoulders top indicates a reversal of an uptrend and is considered bearish. A head-and-shoulders bottom is the reversal of a downtrend and is considered bullish.
hedge	A position taken in a security to offset or reduce the risk associated with the risk of a price change in the commodity or in another security.

I

initial margin	The amount of the good faith deposit that must be deposited in an account when a futures position is established. Also known as original margin.
in the money	A relationship between the strike price of an option and the underlying security's price. A call is in the money when the strike price is lower than the security's price. A put is in the money when the strike price is higher than the security's price.
intrinsic value	The amount by which an option is in the money.
introducing broker (IB)	An individual or organization that solicits or accepts customer orders for futures and options on futures. The introducing broker may not accept checks made out in its name.
inverted market	*See* backwardation.

L

large position report	A report required to be filed in order to prevent large investors from manipulating the price of commodities futures or the value of the underlying cash commodity. The exchanges have set both reporting and maximum limits for the size of a position established on the same side of the market.
last notice day	The last day during the delivery period on which a seller of a futures contract may tender notice of intention to deliver the underlying commodity. Also known as final notice day.
last trading day	The final day when contract for a particular delivery month trades.
leverage transaction merchant or LTM	A person who is required to register or is registered as a leverage transaction merchant under the Act and Commission Rules.
limit order	An order that sets a maximum price that the investor will pay in the case of a buy order or the minimum price the investor will accept in the case of a sell order.
limit up/limit down	The maximum amount by which a contract may rise or fall during a particular trading day based on the previous day's settlement price.
liquidation	The execution of an offsetting sell order to eliminate a long futures contract position.
liquidity	The ability of an investment to be readily converted into cash.
local	*See* floor trader.
long	A term used to describe an investor who owns a futures contract.
long the basis	A term used to describe someone who owns the underlying cash commodity.

M

maintenance call	A demand for additional cash or collateral made by a merchant when a margin customer's account equity has fallen below the minimum requirement.
maintenance margin	The minimum amount of equity that must be maintained in an account to hold an open futures contract position.
margin	The amount of customer equity that is required to hold a position in a futures contract. Sometimes used to describe the amount of equity a customer has in their account.
margin call	A demand for additional cash sent by a firm when the equity in a customer's account has fallen below the minimum required equity.

Market if touched order or MIT	An order where the investor wants the order be executed if the market trades at or through a set price. Unlike a limit order, the MIT order becomes a market order to purchase or sell the contracts at the next available price.
market-on-open/market-on-close order	The investor wants their order executed on the opening of the market or as reasonably close to the opening as practical. The exchange sets an opening time range that is considered to be the open of the trading day.
market order	A market order will guarantee that the investor's order is executed as soon as the order is presented to the market. A market order to either buy or sell guarantees the execution, but not the price at which the order will be executed.
member	A member of NFA other than a contract market.
minimum price variation	The minimum amount by which the price of a commodity may change from the previous trade. Also known as a tick.

N

NFA	The National Futures Association is the SRO for the futures industry. Its main areas of focus are:
	To ensure ethical behavior
	To ensure individuals meet minimum training and knowledge standards
	To ensure firms meet minimum financial standards
	To conduct unannounced spot audits of members
nominal account size	The account size the client agrees to establish to determine the level of trading in the particular trading program.
notice day	*See* first notice day.
notice of delivery	The notice tendered by a clearinghouse, used to inform the broker representing a long contract holder that the short contract holder intends to make physical delivery of the commodity.

O

offer	A price published at which an investor or merchant is willing to sell a futures contract.
offset	The closing out of an open futures position.
omnibus account	An account used by an introducing member to execute and clear all of its customers' trades.

opening range	The exchange sets an opening time range that is considered to be the open of the trading day. All orders executed during this time will be considered to have been executed on the open.
open interest	The number of outstanding futures contracts that have not been offset or closed by investors. The greater the open interest, the greater the liquidity.
open order	An order that is in the hands of the merchant to be executed when the market reaches the terms specified by the order.
open trade equity (OTE)	The total cash value of a futures position based on the initial margin deposit plus or minus any unrealized gains or losses.
option	A commodity futures option is a contract between two parties that determines the time and price at which a futures contract may be bought or sold.
original margin	*See* initial margin.
out of the money	The relationship of an option's strike price to the underlying security's price when exercising the option would not make economic sense. A call is out of the money when the security's price is below the option's strike price. A put is out of the money when the security's price is above the option's strike price.
overbought	A technical condition where the price of the commodity has risen to unsustainable levels and has exhausted all potential buyers.
oversold	A technical condition where the price of the commodity has fallen to unsustainable levels and has exhausted all potential sellers.

P

person	Any natural person or entity that may enter into a legally binding contract and includes individuals, corporations, limited liability companies, partnerships, trusts, associations, and other entities.
pit	The area designated on the floor of a commodities exchange where all transactions in a particular commodity must take place.
position limit	The maximum number of contracts that a person may hold on the same side of the market. Limits are established to prevent large investors from manipulating the price of commodities.
premium	The increased price paid for the delivery of a superior grade of a commodity.
premium market	*See* carrying charge market.
put	A put option gives the buyer the right to sell or to put the futures contract to the seller at a specific price for a certain period of time. The sale of a put option obligates the seller to buy the futures contract from the buyer at that specific price for a certain period of time.
pyramiding	A trading strategy using the unrealized profits on a position to increase the size of the profitable position.

R

range	The difference between the high and low prices of a commodity during any given trading period.
reporting level	The number of contracts established on the same side of the market that triggers the requirement for the holder to file daily position reports. The reporting level is lower than the maximum position limit. Sometimes known as position reporting level.
requirements	As established by the NFA, CFTC, or any exchange are any duty, restriction, procedure, or standard imposed by a charter, rule, bylaw, or regulation.
resistance	A price level to which a futures contract appreciates and attracts sellers. The new sellers keep the security's price from rising any higher.
resting order	*See* open order and limit order.
round turn	The establishment and subsequent offset of a futures contract position. Most FCMs charge commissions based on round turns.

S

scale order	This order is entered when an investor wishes to establish or offset a position by purchasing or selling futures contracts at specified intervals. This will allow an investor to establish or liquidate a position at an average price instead of just executing the full order at a prevailing price.
scalper	A trader who seeks to earn quick profits from small changes in the price of a futures contract. Scalpers are usually floor traders, also known as locals.
settlement price	The official closing price of a futures contract established by the exchange and used to determine the unrealized profit and loss on an open contract position and to determine the change in price in the futures contract for the next session.
short	A position established by a bearish investor in the hopes that the price of the futures contract will fall.
short hedge	The sale of a futures contract to protect a long position in the cash commodity from a decline in price.
short the basis	A term used to describe someone who needs, but who has not yet obtained, the physical cash commodity to effect delivery or to operate a business.
speculator	The objective of the speculator is to make a profit based on their belief about the future price action of a commodity.
spot market	The cash market for a commodity where the physical exchange of the commodity and payments are made for immediate delivery.

spot price	The current price at which the physical commodity may be bought and sold in the cash market.
spread	(1) The difference between the bid and ask for a futures contract. (2) The simultaneous purchase and sale of 2 calls or 2 puts on the same underlying futures contract.
stop-loss order	An order that becomes a limit order to buy or sell the stock when the futures contract trades at or through the stop price.
stop order	An order that becomes a market order to buy or sell the stock when the future's contract trades at or through the stop price.
straddle	The simultaneous purchase or sale of a call and a put on the same security with the same strike price and expiration.
strike price	*See* exercise price.
support	The price to which a futures contract will fall and attract new buyers. New buyers entering the market keep the price from falling any lower.
switch order	An order entered by a customer who wishes to roll out the delivery month to continue holding a position in the underlying commodity but who does not want to take or make delivery.

T

technical analysis	A method of analysis that uses past price performance to predict the future performance of a commodity.
tender	Submission of a notice of intention to make delivery.
tick	*See* minimum price variation.
time value	The value of an option that exceeds its intrinsic value or its in-the-money amount.

U

uncovered call/put	The sale of a call option without owning the underlying futures or the sale of a put option without being short the futures. Uncovered positions are also known as naked positions.
underlying commodity	The commodity on which the futures contract is based and in which the contract may be settled.

V

variation margin	The amount of money required to be deposited to return the equity in a futures account to the initial margin requirement.
visible supply	The amount of a commodity that is known to exist and to be readily available for delivery.

W

warehouse	A certified facility where stock of commodities may be stored and where delivery may be accepted.

Index

Made in the USA
Monee, IL
31 October 2020